THE UPTON LETTERS

By

ARTHUR CHRISTOPHER BENSON

SPECIAL NOTE FROM THE PUBLISHER:

In 1905, Arthur Christopher Benson British essayist, poet and author published

The Upton Letters . The book was composed of correspondences between

authors. We have formatted the book for an easy reading experience if you

enjoy historic classic literary work.

Brought to your courtesy of public domain

S.M.B Special Edition

Originally Published in 1905

PREFACE

These letters were returned to me, shortly after the death of the friend to whom they were written, by his widow. It seems that he had been sorting and destroying letters and papers a few days before his wholly unexpected end. "We won't destroy these," he had said to her, holding the bulky packet of my letters in his hand; "we will keep them together. T—— ought to publish them, and, some day, I hope he will." This was not, of course, a deliberate judgement; but his sudden death, a few days later, gives the unconsidered wish a certain sanctity, and I have determined to obey it. Moreover, she who has the best right to decide, desires it. A few merely personal matters and casual details have been omitted; but the main substance is there, and the letters are just as they were written. Such hurried compositions, of course, abound in literary shortcomings, but perhaps they have a certain spontaneity which more deliberate writings do not always possess. I wrote my best, frankest, and liveliest in the letters, because I knew that Herbert would value both the thought and the expression of the thought. And, further, if it is necessary to excuse so speedy a publication, I feel that they are not letters which would gain by being kept. Their interest arises from the time, the circumstance, the occasion that gave them birth, from the books read and criticised, the educational problems discussed; and thus they may form a species of comment on a certain aspect of modern life, and from a definite point of view. But, after all, it is enough for me that he appreciated them, and, if he wished that they should go out to the world, well, let them go! In publishing them I am but obeying a last message of love.

T. B.
MONK'S ORCHARD, UPTON,
Feb. 20, 1905.

THE UPTON LETTERS

MONK'S ORCHARD, UPTON,
Jan. 23, 1904.

MY DEAR HERBERT,—I have just heard the disheartening news, and I write to say that I am sorry toto corde. I don't yet know the full extent of the calamity, the length of your exile, the place, or the conditions under which you will have to live. Perhaps you or Nelly can find time to let me have a few lines about it all? But I suppose there is a good side to it. I imagine that when the place is once fixed, you will be able to live a much freer life than you have of late been obliged to live in England, with less risk and less overshadowing of anxiety. If you can find the right region, renovabitur ut acquila juventus tua; and you will be able to carry out some of the plans which have been so often interrupted here. Of course there will be drawbacks. Books, society, equal talk, the English countryside which you love so well, and, if I may use the expression, so intelligently; they will all have to be foregone in a measure. But fortunately there is no difficulty about money, and money will give you back some of these delights. You will still see your real friends; and they will come to you with the intention of giving and getting the best of themselves and of you, not in the purposeless way in which one drifts into a visit here. You will be able, too, to view things with a certain detachment—and that is a real advantage; for I have sometimes thought that your literary work has suffered from the variety of your interests, and from your being rather too close to them to form a philosophical view. Your love of characteristic points of natural scenery will help you. When you have once grown familiar with the new surroundings, you will penetrate the secret of their charm, as you have done here. You will be able, too, to live a more undisturbed life, not fretted by all the cross-currents which distract a man in his own land, when he has a large variety of ties. I declare I did not know I was so good a rhetorician; I shall end by convincing myself that there is no real happiness to be found except in expatriation!

Seriously, my dear Herbert, I do understand the sadness of the change; but one gets no good by dwelling on the darker side; there are and will be times, I know, of depression. When one lies awake in the morning, before the nerves are braced by contact with the wholesome day; when one has done a tiring piece of work, and is alone, and in that frame of mind when one needs occupation but yet is not brisk enough to turn to the work one loves; in those dreary intervals between one's work, when one is off with the old and not yet on with the new—well I know all the corners of the road, the shadowy cavernous places where the demons lie in wait for one, as they do for the wayfarer (do you remember?), in Bewick, who, desiring to rest by the roadside, finds the dingle all alive with ambushed fiends, horned and heavy-limbed, swollen with the oppressive clumsiness of nightmare. But you are not inexperienced or weak. You have enough philosophy to wait until the frozen mood thaws, and the old thrill comes back. That is one of the real compensations of middle age. When one is young, one imagines that any depression will be continuous; and one sees the dreary, uncomforted road winding ahead over bare hills, till it falls to the dark valley. But later on one can believe that "the roadside dells of rest" are there, even if one cannot see them; and, after all, you have a home which goes with you; and it would seem to be fortunate, or to speak more truly, tenderly prepared, that you have only daughters—a son, who would have to go back to England to be educated, would be a source of anxiety. Yet I find myself even wishing that you had a son, that I might have the care of him over here. You don't know the heart-hunger I sometimes have for young things of my own to watch over; to try to guard their happiness. You would say that I had plenty of opportunities in my profession; it is true in a sense, and I think I am perhaps a better schoolmaster for being unmarried. But these boys are not one's own; they drift away; they come back dutifully and affectionately to talk to their old tutor; and we are both of us painfully conscious that we have lost hold of the thread, and that the nearness of the tie that once existed exists no more.

Well, I did not mean in this letter to begin bemoaning my own sorrows, but rather to try and help you to bear your own. Tell me as soon as you can what your plans are, and I will come down and see you for the last time under the old conditions; perhaps the new will be happier. God bless you, my old friend! Perhaps the light which has hitherto shone (though fitfully) ON your life will now begin to shine THROUGH it instead; and let me add one word. My assurance grows firmer, from day to day, that we are in stronger hands than our own. It is true that I see things in other lives which look as if those hands were wantonly cruel, hard, unloving; but I reflect that I cannot see all the conditions; I can only humbly fall back upon my own experience, and testify that even the most daunting and humiliating things have a purifying effect; and I can perceive enough at all events to encourage me to send my heart a little farther than my eyes, and to believe that a deep and urgent love is there.—Ever affectionately yours,

T. B.

UPTON,
Jan. 26, 1904.

DEAR HERBERT,—So it is to be Madeira at present? Well, I know Madeira a little, and I can honestly congratulate you. I had feared it might be Switzerland. I could not LIVE in Switzerland. It does me good to go there, to be iced and baked and washed clean with pure air. But the terrible mountains, so cold and unchanged, with their immemorial patience, their frozen tranquillity; the high hamlets, perched on their lonely shelves; the bleak pine-trees, with their indomitable strength—all these depress me. Of course there is much homely beauty among the lower slopes; the thickets, the falling streams, the flowers. But the grim black peaks look over everywhere; and there is seldom a feeling of the rich and comfortable peace such as one gets in England. Madeira is very different. I have been there, and must truthfully confess that it does not suit me altogether—the warm air, the paradisal luxuriance, the greenhouse fragrance, are not a fit setting for a blond, lymphatic man, who pants for Northern winds. But it will suit you; and you will be one of those people, spare and compact as you are, who find themselves vigorous and full of energy there. I have many exquisite vignettes from Madeira which linger in my mind. The high hill-villages, full of leafy trees; the grassy downs at the top; the droop of creepers, full of flower and fragrance, over white walls; the sapphire sea, under huge red cliffs. You will perhaps take one of those embowered Quintas high above the town, in a garden full of shelter and fountains. And I am much mistaken if you do not find yourself in a very short time passionately attached to the place. Then the people are simple, courteous, unaffected, full of personal interest. Housekeeping has few difficulties and no terrors.

I can't get away for a night; but I will come and dine with you one day this week, if you can keep an evening free.

And one thing I will promise—when you are away, I will write to you as often as I can. I shall not attempt any formal letters, but I shall begin with anything that is in my mind, and stop when I feel disposed; and you must do the same. We won't feel bound to ANSWER each other's letters; one wastes time over that. What I shall want to know is what you are thinking and doing, and I shall take for granted you desire the same.

You will be happier, now that you KNOW; I need not add that if I can be of any use to you in making suggestions, it will be a real pleasure.—Ever yours,

T. B.

UPTON,
Feb. 3, 1904.

MY DEAR HERBERT,—It seems ages since we said good-bye—yet it is not a week ago. And now I have been at work all day correcting exercises, teaching, talking. I have had supper with the boys, and I have been walking about since and talking to them—the nicest part of my work. They are at this time of the day, as a rule, in good spirits, charitable, sensible. What an odd thing it is that boys are so delightful when they are alone, and so tiresome (not always) when they are together. They seem, in public, to want to show their worst side, to be ashamed of being supposed to be good, or interested, or thoughtful, or tender-hearted. They are so afraid of seeming better than they are, and pleased to appear worse than they are. I wonder why this is? It is the same more or less with most people; but one sees instincts at their nakedest among boys. As I go on in life, the one thing I desire is simplicity and reality; pose is the one fatal thing. The dullest person becomes interesting if you feel that he is really himself, that he is not holding up some absurd shield or other in front of his shivering soul. And yet how hard it is, even when one appreciates the benefits and beauty of sincerity, to say what one really thinks, without reference to what one supposes the person one is talking to would like or expect one to think—and to do it, too, without brusqueness or rudeness or self-assertion.

Boys are generally ashamed of saying anything that is good about each other; and yet they are as a rule intensely anxious to be POPULAR, and pathetically unaware that the shortest cut to popularity is to see the good points in every one and not to shrink from mentioning them. I once had a pupil, a simple-minded, serene, ordinary creature, who attained to extraordinary popularity. I often wondered why; after he had left, I asked a boy to tell me; he thought for a moment, and then he said, "I suppose, sir, it was because when we were all talking about other chaps—and one does that nearly all the time—he used to be as much down on them as any one else, and he never jawed—but he always had something nice to say about them, not made up, but as if it just came into his head."

Well, I must stop; I suppose you are forging out over the Bay, and sleeping, I hope, like a top. There is no sleep like the sleep on a steamer—profound, deep, so that one wakes up hardly knowing where or who one is, and in the morning you will see the great purple league-long rollers. I remember them; I generally felt very unwell; but there was something tranquillising about them, all the same—and then the mysterious steamers that used to appear alongside, pitching and tumbling, with the little people moving about on the decks; and a mile away in a minute. Then the water in the wake, like marble, with its white-veined sapphire, and the hiss and smell of the foam; all that is very pleasant. Good night, Herbert!—Ever yours,

T. B.

UPTON,
Feb. 9, 1904.

MY DEAR HERBERT,—I hope you have got Lockhart's Life of Scott with you; if not, I will send it out to you. I have been reading it lately, and I have a strong wish that you should do the same. It has not all the same value; the earlier part, the account of the prosperous years, is rather tiresome in places. There is something boisterous, undignified—even, I could think, vulgar—about the aims and ambitions depicted. It suggests a prosperous person, seated at a well-filled table, and consuming his meat with a hearty appetite. The desire to stand well with prominent persons, to found a family, to take a place in the county, is a perfectly natural and wholesome desire; but it is a commonplace ambition. There is a charm in the simplicity, the geniality, the childlike zest of the man; but there is nothing great about it. Then comes the crash; and suddenly, as though a curtain drew up, one is confronted with the spectacle of an indomitable and unselfish soul, bearing a heavy burden with magnificent tranquillity, and settling down with splendid courage to an almost intolerable task. The energy displayed by our hero in attempting to write off the load of debt that hung round his neck is superhuman, august. We see him completing in a single day what would take many writers a week to finish, and doing it day by day, with bereavements, sorrows, ill-health, all closing in upon him. The quality of the work he thus did matters little; it was done, indeed, at a time of life when under normal circumstances he would probably have laid his pen down. But the spectacle of the man's patient energy and divine courage is one that goes straight to the heart. It is then that one realises that the earlier and more prosperous life has all the value of contrast; one recognises that here was a truly unspoilt nature; and that, if we can dare to look upon life as an educative process, the tragic sorrows that overwhelmed him were not the mere reversal of the wheel of fortune, but gifts from the very hand of the Father—to purify a noble soul from the dross that was mingled with it; to give a great man the opportunity of living in a way that should furnish an eternal and imperishable example.

I do not believe that in the whole of literature there is a more noble and beautiful document of its kind than the diary of these later years. The simplicity, the sincerity of the man stand out on every page. There are no illusions about himself or his work. He hears that Southey has been speaking of him and his misfortunes with tears, and he says plainly that such tears would be impossible to himself in a parallel case; that his own sympathy has always been practical rather than emotional; his own tendency has been to help rather than to console. Again, speaking of his own writings, he says that he realises that if there is anything good about his poetry or prose, "It is a hurried frankness of composition, which pleases soldiers, sailors, and young people of bold and active disposition." He adds, indeed, a contemptuous touch to the above, which he was great enough to have spared: "I have been no sigher in shades—no writer of

Songs and sonnets and rustical roundelays
Framed on fancies and whistled on reeds."

A few days later, speaking of Thomas Campbell, the poet, he says that "he has suffered by being too careful a corrector of his work."

That is a little ungenerous, a little complacent; noble and large as Scott's own unconsidered writings are, he ought to have been aware that methods differ. What, for instance, could be more extraordinary than the contrast between Scott and Wordsworth—Scott with his "You know I don't care a curse about what I write;" and Wordsworth, whose chief reading in later days was his own poetry. Whenever the two are brought into actual juxtaposition, Wordsworth is all pose and self-absorption; Scott all simplicity and disregard of fame. Wordsworth staying at Abbotsford declines to join an expedition of pleasure, and stays at home with his daughter. When the party return, they find Wordsworth sitting and being read to by his daughter, the book his own Excursion. A party of travellers arrive, and Wordsworth steals down to the chaise, to see if there are any of his own volumes among the books they have with them. When the two are together, Scott is all courteous deference; he quotes Wordsworth's poems, he pays him stately compliments, which the bard receives as a matter of course, with stiff, complacent bows. But, during the whole of the time, Wordsworth never lets fall a single syllable from which one could gather that he was aware that his host had ever put pen to paper.

Yet, while one desires to shake Wordsworth to get some of his pomposity out of him, one half desires that Scott had felt a little more deeply the dignity of his vocation. One would wish to have infused Wordsworth with a little of Scott's unselfish simplicity, and to have put just a little stiffening into Scott. He ought to have felt—and he did not—that to be a great writer was a more dignified thing than to be a sham seigneur.

But through the darkening scene, when the woods whisper together, and Tweed runs hoarsely below, the simple spirit holds uncomplaining and undaunted on his way: "I did not like them to think that I could ever be beaten by anything," he says. But at length the hand, tired with the pen, falls, and twilight creeps upon the darkening mind.

I paid a pious pilgrimage last summer, as you perhaps remember, to Abbotsford. I don't think I ever described it to you. My first feeling was one of astonishment at the size and stateliness of the place, testifying to a certain imprudent prosperity. But the sight of the rooms themselves; the desk, the chair, the book-lined library, the little staircase by which, early or late, Scott could steal back to his hard and solitary work; the death-mask, with its pathetic smile; the clothes, with hat and shoes, giving, as it were, a sense of the very shape and stature of the man—these brought the whole thing up with a strange reality.

Of course, there is much that is pompous, affected, unreal about the place; the plaster beams, painted to look like oak; the ugly emblazonries; the cruel painted glass; the laboriously collected objects—all these reveal the childish side of Scott, the superficial self which slipped from him so easily when he entered into the cloud.

And then the sight of his last resting-place; the ruined abbey, so deeply embowered in trees that the three dim Eildon peaks are invisible; the birds singing in the thickets that clothe the ruined cloisters—all this made a parable, and brought before one with an intensity of mystery the wonder of it all. The brief life, so full of plans for permanence; the sombre valley of grief; the quiet end, when with failing lips he murmured that the only comfort for the dying heart was the thought that it had desired goodness, however falteringly, above everything.

I can't describe to you how deeply all this affects me—with what a hunger of the heart, what tenderness, what admiration, what wonder. The very frankness of the surprise with which, over and over again, the brave spirit confesses that he does not miss the delights of life as much as he expected, nor find the burden as heavy as he had feared, is a very noble and beautiful thing. I can conceive of no book more likely to make a spirit in the grip of sorrow and failure more gentle, hopeful, and brave; because it brings before one, with quiet and pathetic dignity, the fact that no fame, no success, no recognition, can be weighed for a moment in the balance with those simple qualities of human nature which the humblest being may admire, win, and display.—Ever yours,

T. B.

UPTON,
Shrove Tuesday, Feb. 16, 1904.

DEAR HERBERT,—One of those incredible incidents has just happened here, an incident that makes one feel how little one knows of human beings, and that truth, in spite of the conscientious toil of Mr. H. G. Wells, does still continue to keep ahead of fiction. Here is the story. Some money is missed in a master's house; circumstances seem to point to its having been abstracted by one of the boys. A good-natured, flighty boy is suspected, absolutely without reason, as it turns out; though he is the sort of boy to mislay his own books and other portable property to any extent, and to make no great difficulty under pressure of immediate need, and at the last moment, about borrowing some one else's chattels. On this occasion the small boys in the house, of whom he is one, solemnly accuse him of the theft, and the despoiled owner entreats that the money may be returned. He protests that he has not taken it. The matter comes to the ears of the house-master, who investigates the matter in the course of the evening, and interviews the supposed culprit. The boy denies it again quite unconcernedly and frankly, goes away from the interview, and wandering about, finds the small boys of the house assembled in one of the studies discussing a matter with great interest. "What has happened?" says our suspected friend. "Haven't you heard?" says one of them; "Campbell's grandmother" (Campbell is another of the set) "has sent him a tip of L2." "Oh, has she?" says the boy, with a smile of intense meaning; "I shall have to go my rounds again." This astonishing confession of his guilt is received with the interest it deserves, and Campbell is advised to lock up his money, or to hand it over to the custody of the house-master. In the course of the evening another amazing event occurs; the boy whose money was stolen finds the whole of it, quite intact, in the pocket of his cricketing flannels, where he now remembers having put it. The supposed culprit is restored to favour, and becomes a reliable member of society. One of the small boys tells the matron the story of our hero's amazing remark on the subject, in his presence. The matron stares at him, bewildered, and asks him what made him say it. "Oh, only to rag them," says the boy; "they were all so excited about it." "But don't you see, you silly boy," says the kind old dame, "that if the money had not been found, you would have been convicted out of your own mouth of having been the thief?" "Oh yes," says the boy cheerfully; "but I couldn't help it—it came into my head."

Of course this is an exceptional case; but it illustrates a curious thing about boys—I mentioned it the other day—which is, their extraordinary willingness and even anxiety to be thought worse than they are. Even boys of unexceptionable principle will talk as if they were not only not particular, but positively vicious. They don't like aspersions on their moral character to be made by others, but they rejoice to blacken themselves; and not even the most virtuous boys can bear to be accused of virtue, or thought to be what is called "Pi." This does not happen when boys are by themselves; they will then talk unaffectedly about their principles and practice, if their interlocutor is also unaffected. But when they are together, a kind of disease of self-accusation attacks them. I suppose that it is the perversion of a wholesome instinct, the desire not to be thought better than they are; but part of the exaggerated stories that one hears about the low moral tone of public schools arises from the fact that innocent boys coming to a public school infer, and not unreasonably, from the talk of their companions that they are by no means averse to evil, even when, as is often the case, they are wholly untainted by it.

The same thing seems to me to prevail very widely nowadays. The old-fashioned canting hypocrisy, like that of the old servant in the Master of Ballantrae, who, suffering under the effects of drink, bears himself like a Christian martyr, has gone out; just as the kind of pride is extinct against which the early Victorian books used to warn children, and which was manifested by sitting in a carriage surveying a beggar with a curling lip—a course of action which was invariably followed by the breaking of a Bank, or by some mysterious financial operation involving an entire loss of fortune and respectability.

Nowadays the parable of the Pharisee and the publican is reversed. The Pharisee tells his friends that he is in reality far worse than the publican, while the publican thanks God that he is not a Pharisee. It is only, after all, a different kind of affectation, and perhaps even more dangerous, because it passes under the disguise of a virtue. We are all miserable sinners, of course; but it is no encouragement to goodness if we try to reduce ourselves all to the same level of conscious corruption. The only advantage would be if, by our humility, we avoided censoriousness. Let us frankly admit that our virtues are inherited, and that any one who had had our chances would have done as well or better than ourselves; neither ought we to be afraid of expressing our admiration of virtue, and, if necessary, our abhorrence of vice, so long as that abhorrence is genuine. The cure for the present state of things is a greater naturalness. Perhaps it would end in a certain increase of priggishness; but I honestly confess that nowadays our horror of priggishness, and even of seriousness, has grown out of all proportion; the command not to be a prig has almost taken its place in the Decalogue. After all, priggishness is often little more than a failure in tact, a breach of good manners; it is priggish to be superior, and it is vulgar to let a consciousness of superiority escape you. But it is not priggish to be virtuous, or to have a high artistic standard, or to care more for masterpieces of literature than for second-rate books, any more than it is priggish to be rich or well-connected. The priggishness comes in when you begin to compare yourself with others, and to draw distinctions. The Pharisee in the parable was a prig; and just as I have known priggish hunting men, and priggish golfers, and even priggish card-players, so I have known people who were priggish about having a low standard of private virtue, because they disapproved of people whose standard was higher. The only cure is frankness and simplicity; and one should practise the art of talking simply and directly among congenial people of what one admires and believes in.

How I run on! But it is a comfort to write about these things to some one who will understand; to "cleanse the stuff'd bosom of the perilous stuff that weighs upon the heart." By the way, how careless the repetition of "stuff'd" "stuff" is in that line! And yet it can't be unintentional, I suppose?

I enjoy your letters very much; and I am glad to hear that you are beginning to "take interest," and are already feeling better. Your views of the unchangeableness of personality are very surprising; but I must think them over for a little; I will write about them before long. Meanwhile, my love to you all.—Ever yours,

T. B.

UPTON,
Feb. 25, 1904.

DEAR HERBERT,—You ask what I have been reading. Well, I have been going through Newman's Apologia for the twentieth time, and as usual have fallen completely under the magical spell of that incomparable style; its perfect lucidity, showing the very shape of the thought within, its simplicity (not, in Newman's case, I think, the result of labour, but of pure instinctive grace), its appositeness, its dignity, its music. I oscillate between supreme contentment as a reader, and envious despair as a writer; it fills one's mind up slowly and richly, as honey fills a vase from some gently tilted bowl. There is no sense of elaborateness about the book; it was written swiftly and easily out of a full heart; then it is such a revelation of a human spirit, a spirit so innocent and devoted and tender, and, moreover, charged with a sweet naive egotism as of a child. It was written, as Newman himself said, IN TEARS; but I do not think they were tears of bitterness, but a half-luxurious sorrow, the pathos of the past and its heavinesses, viewed from a quiet haven. I have no sympathy whatever with the intellectual attitude it reveals, but as Roderick Hudson says, I don't always heed the sense: it is indeed a somewhat melancholy spectacle of a beautiful mind converted in reality by purely aesthetic considerations, by the dignity, the far-off, holy, and venerable associations of the great Church which drew him quietly in, while all the time he is under the impression that it is a logical clue which he is following. And what logic! leaping lightly over difficult places, taking flowery by-paths among the fields, the very stairs on which he treads based on all kinds of wide assumptions and unverifiable hypotheses. Then it is distressing to see his horror of Liberalism, of speculation, of development, of all the things that constitute the primal essence of the very religion that he blindly followed. One cannot help feeling that had Newman been a Pharisee, he would have been, with his love of precedent, and antiquity, and tradition, one of the most determined and deadly opponents of the spirit of Christ. For the spirit of Christ is the spirit of freedom, of elasticity, of unconventionality. Newman would have upheld in the Sanhedrim with pathetic and exquisite eloquence that it was not time to break with the old, that it was miserable treachery to throw over the ancient safeguards of faith, to part with the rich inheritance of the national faith delivered by Abraham and Moses to the saints. Newman was a true fanatic, and the most dangerous of fanatics, because his character was based on innocence and tenderness and instinctive virtue. It is rather pathetic than distressing to see Newman again and again deluded by the antiquity of some petty human logician into believing his utterance to be the very voice of God. The struggle with Newman was not the struggle of faith with scepticism, but the struggle between two kinds of loyalty, the personal loyalty to his own past and his own friends and the Church of his nativity, and the loyalty to the infinitely more ancient and venerable tradition of the Roman Church. It was, as I have said, an aesthetic conversion; he had the mind of a poet, and the particular kind of beauty which appealed to him was not the beauty of nature or art, but the beauty of old tradition and the far-off dim figures of saints and prelates reaching back into the dark and remote past.

He had, too, the sublime egotism of the poet. His own salvation—"Shall I be safe if I die to-night?"—that, he confesses, was the thought which eventually outweighed all others. He had little of the priestly hunger to save souls; the way in which others trusted him, confided in him, watched his movements, followed him, was always something of a terror to him, and yet in another mood it ministered to his self-absorption. He had not the stern sense of being absolutely in the right, which is the characteristic of the true leaders of men, but he had a deep sense of his own importance, combined with a perfectly real sense of weakness and humility, which even disguised, I would think, his own egotism from himself.

Again his extraordinary forensic power, his verbal logic, his exquisite lucidity of statement, all these concealed from him, as they have concealed from others, his lack of mental independence. He had an astonishing power of submitting to his imagination, a power of believing the impossible, because the exercise of faith seemed to him so beautiful a virtue. It is not a case of a noble mind overthrown, but of the victory of a certain kind of poetical feeling over all rational inquiry.

To revert to Newman's literary genius, he seems to me to be one of the few masters of English prose. I used to think, in old University days, that Newman's style was best tested by the fact that if one had a piece of his writing to turn into Latin prose, the more one studied it, turned it over, and penetrated it, the more masterly did it become; because it was not so much the expression of a thought as the thought itself taking shape in a perfectly pure medium of language. Bunyan had the same gift; of later authors Ruskin had it very strongly, and Matthew Arnold in a lesser degree. There is another species of beautiful prose, the prose of Jeremy Taylor, of Pater, even of Stevenson; but this is a slow and elaborate construction, pinched and pulled this way and that; and it is like some gorgeous picture, of stately persons in seemly and resplendent dress, with magnificently wrought backgrounds of great buildings and curious gardens. But the work of Newman and of Ruskin is a white art, like the art of sculpture.

I find myself every year desiring and admiring this kind of lucidity and purity more and more. It seems to me that the only function of a writer is to express obscure, difficult, and subtle thoughts easily. But there are writers, like Browning and George Meredith, who seem to hold it a virtue to express simple thoughts obscurely. Such writers have a wide vogue, because so many people do not value a thought unless they can feel a certain glow of satisfaction in having grasped it; and to have disentangled a web of words, and to find the bright thing lying within, gives them a pleasing feeling of conquest, and, moreover, stamps the thought in their memory. But such readers have not the root of the matter in them; the true attitude is the attitude of desiring to apprehend, to progress, to feel. The readers who delight in obscurity, to whom obscurity seems to enhance the value of the thing apprehended, are mixing with the intellectual process a sort of acquisitive and commercial instinct very dear to the British heart. These bewildering and bewildered Browning societies who fling themselves upon Sordello, are infected unconsciously with a virtuous craving for "taking higher ground." Sordello contains many beautiful things, but by omitting the necessary steps in argument, and by speaking of one thing allusively in terms of another, and by a profound desultoriness of thought, the poet produces a blurred and tangled impression. The beauties of Sordello would not lose by being expressed coherently and connectedly.

This is the one thing that I try with all my might to impress on boys; that the essence of all style is to say what you mean as forcibly as possible; the bane of classical teaching is that the essence of successful composition is held to be to "get in" words and phrases; it is not a bad training, so long as it is realised to be only a training, in obtaining a rich and flexible vocabulary, so that the writer has a choice of words and the right word comes at call. But this is not made clear in education, and the result on many minds is that they suppose that the essence of good writing is to search diligently for sparkling words and sonorous phrases, and then to patch them into a duller fabric.

But I stray from my point: all paths in a schoolmaster's mind lead out upon the educational plain.

All that you tell me of your new surroundings is intensely interesting. I am thankful that you feel the characteristic charm of the place, and that the climate seems to suit you. You say nothing of your work; but I suppose that you have had no time as yet. The mere absorbing of new impressions is a fatiguing thing, and no good work can be done until a scene has become familiar. I will discharge your commissions punctually; don't hesitate to tell me what you want. I don't do it from a sense of duty, but it is a positive pleasure for me to have anything to do for you. I long for letters; as soon as possible send me photographs, and not merely inanimate photographs of scenes and places, but be sure that you make a part of them yourself. I want to see you standing, sitting, reading in the new house; and give me an exact and detailed account of your day, please; the food you eat, the clothes you wear; you know my insatiable appetite for trifles.— Ever yours,

T. B.

UPTON,
March 5, 1904.

MY DEAR HERBERT,—I have been thinking over your last letter: and by the merest chance I stumbled yesterday on an old diary; it was in 1890—a time, do you remember, when our paths had drifted somewhat apart; you had just married, and I find a rather bitter entry, which it amuses me to tell you of now, to the effect that the marriage of a friend, which ought to give one a new friend, often simply deprives one of an old one—"nec carus aeque nec superstes integer," I add. Then I was, I suppose, hopelessly absorbed in my profession; it was at the time when I had just taken a boarding-house, and suffered much from the dejection which arises from feeling unequal to the new claims.

It amuses me now to think that I could ever have thought of losing your friendship; and it was only temporary; it was only that we were fully occupied; you had to learn camaraderie with your wife, for want of which one sees dryness creep into married lives, when the first divine ardours of passion have died away, and when life has to be lived in the common light of day. Well, all that soon adjusted itself; and then I, too, found in your wife a true and congenial friend, so that I can honestly say that your marriage has been one of the most fortunate events of my life.

But that was not what I meant to write to you about; the point is this. You say that personality is a stubborn thing. It is indeed. I find myself reflecting and considering how much one's character really changes as life goes on; in reading this diary of fourteen years ago, though I have altered in some superficial respects, I was confronted with my unalterable self. I have acquired certain aptitudes; I have learnt, for instance, to understand boys better, to sympathise with them, to put myself in their place, to manage them. I don't think I could enunciate my technique, such as it is. If a young master, just entering upon the work of a boarding-house, asked my advice, I could utter several maxims which he would believe (and rightly) to be the flattest and most obvious truisms; but the value of them to me is that they are deduced from experience, and not stated as assumptions. The whole secret lies in the combination of them, the application of them to a particular case; it is not that one sees a thing differently, but that one knows instinctively the sort of thing to say, the kind of line to pursue, the kind of statement that appeals to a boy as sensible and memorable, the sort of precautions to take, the delicate adjustment of principles to a particular case, and so forth. It is, I suppose, something like the skill of an artist; he does not see nature more clearly, if indeed as clearly, as he did when he began, but he knows better what kind of stroke and what kind of tint will best produce the effect which he wishes to record. Of course both artist and schoolmaster get mannerised; and I should be inclined to say in the latter case that a schoolmaster's success (in the best sense) depends almost entirely upon his being able to arrive at sound principles and at the same time to avoid mannerism in applying them. For instance, it is of no use to hold up for a boy's consideration a principle which is quite outside his horizon; what one has to do is to try and give him a principle which is just a little ahead of his practice, which he can admire and also believe to be within his reach.

Besides this experience which I have acquired, I have acquired a similar experience in the direction of teaching—I know now the sort of statement which arrests the attention and arouses the interest of boys; I know how to put a piece of knowledge so that it appears both intelligible and also desirable to acquire.

Then I have learnt, in literary matters, the art of expression to a certain extent. I can speak to you with entire frankness and unaffectedness, and I will say that I am conscious that I can now express lucidly, and to a certain extent attractively, an idea. My deficiency is now in ideas and not in the power of expressing them. I have quality though not quantity. It amuses me to read this old diary and see how impossible I found it to put certain thoughts into words.

But apart from these definite acquirements, I cannot see that my character has altered in the smallest degree. I detect the same little, hard, repellent core of self, sitting enthroned, cold, unchanging, and unchanged, "like a toad within a stone," to borrow Rossetti's great simile. I see exactly the same weaknesses, the same pitiful ambitions, the same faults. I have learnt, I think, to conceal them a little better; but they are not eradicated, nor even modified. Even with regard to their concealment, I have a terrible theory. I believe that the faults of which one is conscious, which one admits, and even the faults of which one faintly suspects oneself, and yet supposes that one conceals from the world at large, are the very faults that are absolutely patent to every one else. If one dimly suspects that one is a liar, a coward, or a snob, and gratefully believes that one has not been placed in a position which inevitably reveals these characteristics in their full nakedness, one may be fairly certain that other people know that one is so tainted.

The discouraging point is that one is not similarly conscious of one's virtues. I take for granted that I have some virtues, because I see that most of the people whom I meet have some sprinkling of them, but I declare that I am quite unable to say what they are. A fault is patent and unmistakable. The old temptation comes upon one, and one yields as usual; but with one's virtues, if they ever manifest themselves, one's own feeling is that one might have done better. Moreover, if one tries deliberately to take stock of one's good points, they seem to be only natural and instinctive ways of behaving; to which no credit can possibly attach, because by temperament one is incapable of acting otherwise.

Another melancholy fact which I believe to be true is this—that the only good work one does is work which one finds easy and likes. I have one or two patiently acquired virtues which are not natural to me, such as a certain methodical way of dealing with business; but I never find myself credited with it by others, because it is done, I suppose, painfully and with effort, and therefore unimpressively.

I look round, and the same phenomenon meets me everywhere. I do not know any instance among my friends where I can trace any radical change of character. "Sicut erat in principio et nunc et semper et in saecula saeculorum."

Indeed the only line upon which improvement is possible seems to me to be this—that a man shall definitely commit himself to a course of life in which he shall be compelled to exercise virtues which are foreign to his character, and any lapses of which will be penalised in a straightforward, professional way. If a man, for instance, is irritable, impatient, unpunctual, let him take up some line where he is bound to be professionally bland, patient, methodical. That would be the act of a philosopher; but, alas, how few of us choose our profession from philosophical motives!

And even so I should fear that the tendencies of temperament are only temporarily imprisoned, and not radically cured; after all, it fits in with the Darwinian theory. The bird of paradise, condemned to live in a country of marshes, cannot hope to become a heron. The most he can hope is that, by meditating on the advantages which a heron would enjoy, and by pressing the same consideration on his offspring, the time may come in the dim procession of years when the beaks of his descendants will grow long and sharp, their necks pliant, their legs attenuated.

And anyhow, one is bound in honour to have a try; and the hopefulness of my creed (you may be puzzled to detect it) lies in the fact that one HAS a sense of honour about it all; that one's faults are repugnant, and that missing virtues are desirable—possunt quia posse videntur!

Thank you for the photographs. I begin to realise your house; but I want some interiors as well; and let me have the view from your terrace, though I daresay it is only sea and sky.—Ever yours,

T. B.

UPTON,
March 15, 1904.

DEAR HERBERT,—You say I am not ambitious enough; well, I wish I could make up my mind clearly on the subject of ambition; it has been brought before me rather acutely lately. A post here has just fallen vacant—a post to which I should have desired to succeed. I have no doubt that if I had frankly expressed my wishes on the subject, if I had even told a leaky, gossipy colleague what I desired, and begged him to keep it to himself, the thing would have got out, and the probability is that the post would have been offered to me. But I held my tongue, not, I confess, from any very high motive, but merely from a natural dislike of being importunate—it does not seem to me consistent with good manners.

Well, I made no sign; and another man was appointed. I have no doubt that a man of the world would say frankly that I was a fool, and, though I am rather inclined to agree with him, I don't think I could have acted otherwise.

I am inclined to encourage ambition of every kind among the boys. I think it is an appropriate virtue for their age and temperament. It is not a Christian virtue; for it is certain that, if one person succeeds in an ambitious prospect, there must be a dozen who are disappointed. But though I don't approve of it on abstract grounds, yet I think it is so tremendous a motive for activity and keenness that it seems to me that boys are the better for it. I don't believe that in education the highest motive is always the best; indeed, the most effective motive, in dealing with immature minds, is the thing which we have to discover and use.

I mean, for instance, that I think it is probably more effective to say to a boy who is disposed to be physically indolent, "You have a chance of getting your colours this half, and I should like to see you get them," than to say, "I don't want you to think about colours. I want you to play football for the glory of God, because it makes you into a stronger, more wholesome, more cheerful man." It seems to me that boys should learn for themselves that there are often better and bigger reasons for having done a thing than the reason that made them do it.

What makes an object seem desirable to a boy is that others desire to have it too, and that he should be the fortunate person to get it. I don't see how the sense of other people's envy and disappointment can be altogether subtracted from the situation—it certainly is one of the elements which makes success seem desirable to many boys—though a generous nature will not indulge the thought.

But I am equally sure that, as one gets older, one ought to put aside such thoughts altogether. That one ought to trample down ambitious desires and even hopes. That glory, according to the old commonplace, ought to follow and not to be followed.

I think one ought to pursue one's own line, to do one's own business to the best of one's ability, and leave the rest to God. If He means one to be in a big place, to do a big work, it will be clearly enough indicated; and the only chance of doing it in a big way is to be simple-minded, sincere, generous, and contented.

The worst of that theory is this. One sees people in later life who have just missed big chances; some over-subtle delicacy of mind, some untimely reticence or frankness, some indolent hanging-back, some scrupulousness, has just checked them from taking a bold step forward when it was needed. And one sees them with large powers, noble capacities, wise thoughts, relegated to the crowd of unconsidered and inconsiderable persons whose opinion has no weight, whose suggestions have no effectiveness. Are they to be blamed? Or has one humbly and faithfully to take it as an indication that they are just not fit, from some secret weakness, some fibre of feebleness, to take the tiller?

I am speaking with entire sincerity when I say to you that I think I am myself rather cast in that mould. I have always just missed getting what used to be called "situations of dignity and emolument," and I have often been condoled with as the person who ought to have had them.

Well, I expect that this is probably a very wholesome discipline for me, but I cannot say that it is pleasant, or that use has made it easier.

The worst of it is that I have an odd mixture of practicality and mysticism within me, and I have sometimes thought that one has damaged the other. My mysticism has pulled me back when I ought to have taken a decided step, urging "Leave it to God"—and then, when I have failed to get what I wanted, my mysticism has failed to comfort me, and the practical side of me has said, "The decided step was what God clearly indicated to you was needed; and you were lazy and would not take it."

I have a highly practical friend, the most absolutely and admirably worldly person I know. In talk he sometimes lets fall very profound maxims. We were talking the other day about this very point, and he said musingly, "It is a very good rule in this world not to ask for anything unless you are pretty sure to get it." That is the cream of the worldly attitude. Such a man is not going to make himself tiresome by importunity. He knows what he desires, he works for it, and, when the moment comes, he just gives the little push that is needed, and steps into his kingdom.

That is exactly what I cannot do. It is not a sign of high-mindedness, for I am by nature greedy, acquisitive, and ambitious. But it is a want of firmness, I suppose. Anyhow, there it is, and one cannot alter one's temperament.

The conclusion which I come to for myself and for all like-minded persons—not a very happy class, I fear—is that one should absolutely steel oneself against disappointment, not allow oneself to indulge in pleasing visions, not form plans or count chickens, but try to lay hold of the things which do bring one tranquillity, the simple joys of ordinary and uneventful life. One may thus arrive at a certain degree of independence. And though the heart may ache a little at the chances missed, yet one may console oneself by thinking that it is happier not to realise an ambition and be disappointed, than to realise it and be disappointed.

It all comes from over-estimating one's own powers, after all. If one is decently humble, no disappointment is possible; and such little successes as one does attain are like gleams of sunlight on a misty day.—Ever yours,

T. B.

UPTON,
March 25, 1904.

DEAR HERBERT,—You are quite right about conventionality in education.

One of my perennial preoccupations here is how to encourage originality and independence among my boys. The great danger of public-school education nowadays, as you say, is the development of a type. It is not at all a bad type in many ways; the best specimens of the public-school type are young men who are generous, genial, unembarrassed, courageous, sensible, and active; but our system all tends to level character, and I do not feel sure whether it levels it up or levels it down. In old days the masters concerned themselves with the work of the boys only, and did not trouble their heads about how the boys amused themselves out of school. Vigorous boys organised games for themselves, and indolent boys loafed. Then it came home to school authorities that there was a good deal of danger in the method; that lack of employment was an undesirable thing. Thereupon work was increased, and, at the same time, the masters laid hands upon athletics and organised them. Side by side with this came a great increase of wealth and leisure in England, and there sprang up that astonishing and disproportionate interest in athletic matters, which is nowadays a real problem for all sensible men. But the result of it all has been that there has grown up a stereotyped code among the boys as to what is the right thing to do. They are far less wilful and undisciplined than they used to be; they submit to work, as a necessary evil, far more cheerfully than they used to do; and they base their ideas of social success entirely on athletics. And no wonder! They find plenty of masters who are just as serious about games as they are themselves; who spend all their spare time in looking on at games, and discuss the athletic prospects of particular boys in a tone of perfectly unaffected seriousness. The only two regions which masters have not organised are the intellectual and moral regions. The first has been tacitly and inevitably extruded. A good deal more work is required from the boys, and unless a boy's ability happens to be of a definite academical order—in which case he is well looked after—there is no loop-hole through which intellectual interest can creep in. A boy's time is so much occupied by definite work and definite games that there is neither leisure nor, indeed, vigour left to follow his own pursuits. Life is lived so much more in public that it becomes increasingly difficult for SETS to exist; small associations of boys with literary tastes used to do a good deal in the direction of fostering the germs of intellectual life; the net result is, that there is now far less interest abroad in intellectual things, and such interests as do exist, exist in a solitary way, and generally mean an intellectual home in the background.

In the moral region, I think we have much to answer for; there is a code of morals among boys which, if it is not actively corrupting, is at least undeniably low. The standard of purity is low; a vicious boy doesn't find his vicious tendencies by any means a bar to social success. Then the code of honesty is low; a boy who is habitually dishonest in the matter of work is not in the least reprobated. I do not mean to say that there are not many boys who are both pure-minded and honest; but they treat such virtues as a secret preference of their own, and do not consider that it is in the least necessary to interfere with the practice of others, or even to disapprove of it. And then comes the perennial difficulty of schoolboy honour; the one unforgivable offence is to communicate anything to masters; and an innocent-minded boy whose natural inclination to purity gave way before perpetual temptation and even compulsion might be thought to have erred, but would have scanty, if any, expression of either sympathy or pity from other boys; while if he breathed the least hint of his miserable position to a master and the fact came out, he would be universally scouted.

This is a horrible fact to contemplate; yet it cannot be cured by enactment, only from within. It is strange that in this respect it is entirely unlike the code of the world. No girl or woman would be scouted for appealing to police protection in similar circumstances; no man would be required to submit to violence or even to burglary; no reprobation would fall upon him if he appealed to the law to help him.

Is it not possible to encourage something of this feeling in a school? Is it not possible, without violating schoolboy honour, which is in many ways a fine and admirable thing, to allow the possibility of an appeal to protection for the young and weak against vile temptations? It seems to me that it would be best if we could get the boys to organise such a system among themselves. But to take no steps to arrive at such an organisation, and to leave matters severely alone, is a very dark responsibility to bear.

It is curious to note that in the matter of bullying and cruelty, which used to be so rife at schools, public opinion among boys does seem to have undergone a change. The vice has practically disappeared, and the good feeling of a school would be generally against any case of gross bullying; but the far more deadly and insidious temptation of impurity has, as far as one can learn, increased. One hears of simply heart-rending cases where a boy dare not even tell his parents of what he endures. Then, too, a boy's relations will tend to encourage him to hold out, rather than to invoke a master's aid, because they are afraid of the boy falling under the social ban.

This is the heaviest burden a schoolmaster has to bear; to be responsible for his boys, and to be held responsible, and yet to be probably the very last person to whom the information of what is happening can possibly come.

One great difficulty seems to be that boys will only, as a rule, combine for purposes of evil. In matters of virtue a boy has to act for himself; and I confess, too, with a sigh, that a set of virtuous boys banding themselves together to resist evil and put it down has an alarmingly priggish sound.

The most that a man can do at present, it seems to me, is to have good sensible servants; to be vigilant and discreet; to try and cultivate a paternal relation with all his boys; to try and make the bigger boys feel some responsibility in the matter; but the worst of it is that the subject is so unpleasant that many masters dare not speak of it at all; and excuse themselves by saying that they don't want to put ideas into boys' heads. I cannot conscientiously believe that a man who has been through a big public school himself can honestly be afraid of that. But we all seem to be so much afraid of each other, of public opinion, of possible unpopularity, that we find excuses for letting a painful thing alone.

But to leave this part of the subject, which is often a kind of nightmare to me, and to return to my former point; I do honestly think it a great misfortune that we tend to produce a type. It seems to me that to aim at independence, to know one's own mind, to form one's own ideas—liberty, in short—is one of the most sacred duties in life. It is not only a luxury in which a few can indulge, it ought to be a quality which every one should be encouraged to cultivate. I declare that it makes me very sad sometimes to see these well-groomed, well-mannered, rational, manly boys all taking the same view of things, all doing the same things, smiling politely at the eccentricity of any one who finds matter for serious interest in books, in art or music: all splendidly reticent about their inner thoughts, with a courteous respect for the formalities of religion and the formalities of work; perfectly correct, perfectly complacent, with no irregularities or angular preferences of their own; with no admiration for anything but athletic success, and no contempt for anything but originality of ideas. They are so nice, so gentlemanly, so easy to get on with; and yet, in another region, they are so dull, so unimaginative, so narrow-minded. They cannot all, of course, be intellectual or cultivated; but they ought to be more tolerant, more just, more wise. They ought to be able to admire vigour and enthusiasm in every department instead of in one or two; and it is we who ought to make them feel so, and we have already got too much to do—though I am afraid that you will think, after reading this vast document, that I, at all events, have plenty of spare time. But it is not the case; only the end of the half is at hand; we have finished our regular work, and I have done my reports, and am waiting for a paper. When you next hear I shall be a free man. I shall spend Easter quietly here; but I have so much to do and clear off that I probably shall not be able to write until I have set off on my travels.—Ever yours,

T. B.

THE RED DRAGON,
COMPTON FEREDAY,
April 10, 1904.

DEAR HERBERT,—I was really too busy to write last week, but I am going to try and make up for it. This letter is going to be a diary. Expect more of it.—T. B.

April 7.—I find myself, after all, compelled to begin my walking tour alone. At the last moment Murchison has thrown me over. His father is ill, and he is compelled to spend his holidays at home. I do not altogether like to set off by myself, but it is too late to try and arrange for another companion. I had rather, however, go by myself than with some one who is not absolutely congenial. One requires on these occasions to have a companion whose horizon is the same as one's own. I daresay I could find an old friend, who is not also a colleague, to go with me, but it would mean a certain amount of talk to bring us into line. Then, too, I have had a very busy term; besides my form work, I have had a good deal of extra teaching to do with the Army Class boys. It is interesting work, for the boys are interested, not in the subjects so much, as in mastering them for examination purposes. Yet it matters little how the interest is obtained, as long as the boys believe in the usefulness of what they are doing. But the result is that I am tired out. I have lived with boys from morning to night, and my spare time has been taken up with working at my subjects. I have had hardly any exercise, and but a scanty allowance of sleep. Now I mean to have both. I shall spend my days in the open air, and I shall sleep, I hope, like a top at nights. Gradually I shall recover my power of enjoyment; for the worst of such weeks as I have been passing through is that they leave one dreary and jaded; one finds oneself in that dull mood when one cannot even realise beautiful things. I hear a thrush sing in a bush, or the sunset flames broadly behind the elms, and I say to myself, "That is very beautiful if only I could feel it to be so!" Boys are exhausting companions—they are so restless, so full-blooded, so pitilessly indifferent, so desperately interested in the narrow round of school life; and I have the sort of temperament that will efface itself to any extent, if only the people that I am concerned with will be content. I suppose it is a feeble trait, and that the best schoolmasters have a magnetic influence over boys which makes the boys interested in the master's subjects, or at least hypnotises them into an appearance of interest. I cannot do that. It is like a leaden weight upon me if I feel that a class is bored; the result is that I arrive at the same end in my own way. I have learnt a kind of sympathy with boys; I know by instinct what will interest them, or how to put a tiresome thing in an interesting way.

But I shudder to think how sick I am of it all! I want a long bath of silence and recollection and repose. I want to fill my cistern again with my own thoughts and my own dreams, instead of pumping up the muddy waters of irrigation. I don't think my colleagues are like that. I sate with half-a-dozen of them last night at supper. They were full of all they meant to do. Two of the most energetic were going off to play golf, and the chief pleasure of the place they were going to was that it was possible to get a round on Sundays; they were going to fill the evening with bridge, and one of them said with heart-felt satisfaction, "I am only going to take two books away with me—one on golf and the other on bridge—and I am going to cure some of my radical faults." I thought to myself that if he had forborne to mention the subjects of his books, one might have supposed that they would be a Thomas-a-Kempis and a Taylor's Holy Living, and then how well it would have seemed! Two more were going for a rapid tour abroad in a steamer chartered for assistant masters. That seemed to me to be almost more depressing. They were going to ancient historical places, full of grave and beautiful associations; places to go to, it seemed to me, with some single like-minded associate, places to approach with leisurely and untroubled mind, with no feeling of a programme or a time-table—and least of all in the company of busy professional people with an academical cicerone.

Still, I suppose that this is true devotion to one's profession. They will be able, they think, to discourse easily and, God help us, picturesquely about what they have seen, to intersperse a Thucydides lesson with local colour, and to describe the site of the temple of Delphi to boys beginning the Eumenides. It is very right and proper, no doubt, but it produces in me a species of mental nausea to think of the conditions under which these impressions will be absorbed. The arrangements for luncheon, the brisk interchange of shop, the cheery comments of fellow-tradesmen, the horrible publicity and banality of the whole affair!

My two other colleagues were going, one to spend a holiday at Brighton—which he said was very bracing at Easter, adding that he expected to fall in with some fellows he knew. They will all stroll on the Parade, smoke cigarettes together, and adjourn for a game of billiards. No doubt a very harmless way of passing the time, but not to me enlivening. But Walters is a conventional person, and, as long as he is doing what he would call "the correct thing," he is perfectly and serenely content. The sixth and last is going to Surbiton to spend the holidays with a mother and three sisters, and I think he is the most virtuously employed of all. He will walk out alone, with a terrier dog, before lunch; and after lunch he will go out with his sisters; and perhaps the vicar will come to tea. But then it will be home, and the girls will be proud of their brother, and will have the dishes he likes, and he will have his father's old study to smoke in. I am not sure that he is not the happiest of all, because he is not only pursuing his own happiness.

But I have no such duties before me. I might, I suppose, go down to my sister Helen at the Somersetshire vicarage where she lives so full a life. But the house is small, there are four children, and not much money, and I should only be in the way. Charles would do his best to welcome me, but he will be in a great fuss over his Easter services; and he will ask me to use his study as though it was my own room, which will necessitate a number of hurried interviews in the drawing-room, my sister will take her letters up to her bedroom, and the doors will have to be carefully closed to exclude my tobacco smoke.

This is all very sordid, no doubt, but I am confronted with sordid things to-day. The boys have just cleared off, and they are beginning to sweep out the schoolrooms. The inky, dreary desks, the ragged books, the odd fives-shoes in the pigeon-holes, the wheelbarrows full of festering orange-peel and broken-down fives-balls: this is not a place for a self-respecting person to be in. I want to be mooning about country lanes, with the smell of spring woods blowing down the valley. I want to be holding slow converse with leisurely rustic persons, to be surveying from the side of a high grassy hill the rich plain below, to hear the song of birds in the thickets, to try and feel myself one with the life of the world instead of a sordid sweeper of a corner of it. This is all very ungrateful to my profession, which I love, but it is a necessary reaction; and what at this moment chiefly makes me grateful to it is that my pocket is full enough to let me have a holiday on a liberal scale, without thinking of small economies. I may give pennies to tramps or children, or a shilling to a sexton for showing me a church. I may travel what class I choose, and put up at a hotel without counting the cost; and oh! the blessedness of that. I would rather have a three-days' holiday thus than three weeks with an anxious calculation of resources.

April 8.—I am really off to the Cotswolds. I packed my beloved knapsack yesterday afternoon. I put in it—precision is the essence of diarising—a spare shirt, which will have to serve if necessary as a nightgown, a pair of socks, a pair of slippers, a toothbrush, a small comb, and a sponge; that is sufficient for a philosopher. A pocket volume of poetry—Matthew Arnold this time—and a map completed my outfit. And I sent a bag containing a more liberal wardrobe to a distant station, which I calculated it would take me three days to reach. Then I went off by an afternoon train, and, by sunset, I found myself in a little town, Hinton Perevale, of stone-built houses, with an old bridge. I had no sense of freedom as yet, only a blessed feeling of repose. I took an early supper in a small low-roofed parlour with mullioned windows. By great good fortune I found myself the only guest at the inn, and had the room to myself; then I went early and gratefully to bed, utterly sleepy and content, with just enough sense left to pray for a fine day.

My prayer is answered this morning. I slept a dreamless sleep, and was roused by the cheerful crowing of cocks, which picked about the back yard of the inn. I dressed quickly, only suspending my task to watch the little dramas of the inn yard—the fowls on the pig-sty wall; the horse waiting meekly, with knotted traces hanging round it, to be harnessed; the cat, on some grave business of its own, squeezing gracefully under a closed barn door; the weary, flat-footed duck, nuzzling the mud of a small pool as delicately as though it were a rich custard. I was utterly free; I might go and come as I liked. Time had ceased to exist for me, and it was pleasant to reflect, as I finished my simple breakfast, that I should under professional conditions have been hurrying briskly into school for an hour of Latin Prose. The incredible absurdity and futility of it all came home to me. Half the boys that I teach so elaborately would be both more wholesomely and happily employed if they were going out to farm-work for the day. But they are gentlemen's sons, and so must enter what are called the liberal professions, to retire at the age of sixty with a poor digestion, a peevish wife, and a family of impossible children. But it is only in such inconsequent moments that I allow myself to think thus slightingly of Latin Prose. It is a valuable accomplishment, and, when I have repaired the breaches made by professional work in the mental equilibrium, I shall rejoin my colleagues with a full sense of its paramount importance.

I scribble this diary with a vile pen, and ink like blacking, on the corner of my breakfast-table. I have packed my knapsack, and in a few minutes I shall set out upon my march.

April 9.—I spent an almost perfect day yesterday. It was a cool bright day, with a few clouds like cotton-wool moving sedately in a blue sky. I first walked quietly about my little town, which was full of delicate beauties. The houses are all built of a soft yellow stone, which weathers into a species of rich orange. Heaven knows where the designers came from, but no two houses seem alike; some of them are gabled, buttressed, stone-mullioned, irregular in outline, but yet with a wonderful sense of proportion. Some are Georgian, with classical pilasters and pediments. Yet they are all for use and not for show; and the weak modern shop-windows, which some would think disfigure the delicate house-fronts, seem to me just to give the requisite sense of contrast. At the end of the street stands the church, with a stately Perpendicular tower, and a resonant bell which tells the hour. This overlooks a pile of irregular buildings, now a farm, but once a great manor-house, with a dovecote and pavilions; but the old terrace is now an orchard, and the fine oriel of the house looks straight into the byre. Inside the church—it is open and well-kept—you can trace the history of the manor and its occupants, from Job Best, a rich mercer of London, whose monument, with marble pillars and obelisks, adorns the south aisle; his son was ennobled, whose effigy—more majestic still, robed and coroneted, with his Viscountess by his side, and her dog (with his name, Jakke, engraven on his shoulder)—lies smiling, the slender hands crossed in prayer. But the house was not destined to survive. The Viscount's only daughter, the Lady Penelope, looks down from the wall, a fair and delicate lady, the last of her brief race, who, as the old inscription says with a tender simplicity, "dyed a mayd." I cannot help wondering, my pretty lady, what your story was; and it will do you no hurt if one, who looks upon your gentle face, sends a wondering message of tenderness behind the veil to your pure spirit, regret for your vanished charm, and the fragrance of your soft bloom, and sadness for all sweet things that fade.

The manor, so I learn, was burnt wantonly by the Roundheads—there was a battle hereabouts—on the charge that it had harboured some followers of the king; and so our dreams of greatness and permanence are fulfilled.

The whole church was very neat and spruce; it had suffered a restoration lately. The walls were stripped of their old plaster and pointed, so that the inside is now rougher than the outside, a thing the ancient builders never intended. The altar is fairly draped with good hangings behind, and the chancel fitted with new oak stalls and seats, all as neat as a new pin. As I lingered in the church, reading the simple monuments, a rosy, burly vicar came briskly in, and seeing me there, courteously showed me all the treasures of his house, like Hezekiah. He took me into the belfry, and there, piled up against the wall, were some splendid Georgian columns and architraves, richly carved in dark brown wood. I asked what it was. "Oh, a horrible pompous thing," he said; "it was behind the altar—most pagan and unsuitable; we had it all out as soon as I came. The first moment I entered the church, I said to myself, 'THAT must go,' and I have succeeded, though it was hard enough to collect the money, and actually some of the old people here objected." I did not feel it was worth while to cast cold water on the good man's satisfaction—but the pity of it! I do not suppose that a couple of thousand pounds could have reproduced it; and it is simply heart-rending to see such a noble monument of piety and careful love sacrificed to a wave of so-called ecclesiastical taste. The vicar's chief pride was a new window, by a fashionable modern firm; quite unobjectionable in design, and with good colour, but desperately uninteresting. It represented some mild, unemphatic, attenuated saints, all exactly alike, languidly and decorously conversing together, weighed down by heavy drapery, as though wrapped in bales of carpets. In the lower compartments knelt some dignified persons, similarly habited, in face exactly like the saints above, except that they were fitted out with unaccountable beards—all pretty and correct, but with no character or force. I suppose that fifty years hence, when our taste has broadened somewhat, this window will probably be condemned as impossible too. There can be no absolute canon of beauty; the only principle ought to be to spare everything that is of careful and solid workmanship, to give it a chance, to let time and age have their perfect work. It is the utter conventionality of the whole thing that is so distressing; the same thing is going on all over the country, the attempt to put back the clock, and to try and restore things as they were; history, tradition, association, are not considered. The old builders were equally ruthless, it is true; they would sweep away a Norman choir to build a Decorated one; but at all events they were advancing and expanding, not feebly recurring to a past period of taste, and trying to obliterate the progress of the centuries.

About noon I left the little town, and struck out up a winding lane to the hills. The copses were full of anemones and primroses; birds sang sharply in the bushes which were gemmed with fresh green; now and then I heard the woodpecker laugh as if at some secret jest among the thickets. Presently the little town was at my feet, looking small and tranquil in the golden noon; and soon I came to the top. It was grassy, open down-land up here, and in an instant the wide view of a rich wooded and watered plain spread before me, with shadowy hills on the horizon. In the middle distance I saw the red roofs of a great town, the smoke going peacefully up; here was a shining river-reach, like a crescent of silver. It was England indeed—tranquil, healthy, prosperous England.

The rest of the day I need not record. It was full of delicate impressions— an old, gabled, mullioned house among its pastures; a hamlet by a stream, admirably grouped; a dingle set with primroses; and over all, the long, pure lines of upland, with here and there, through a gap, the purple, wealthy plain.

I write this in the evening, at a little wayside inn, in a hamlet under the hill. The name alone, Wenge Grandmain, is worth a shilling. It is very simple, but clean, and the people are kind; not with the professional manner of those who bow, smiling, to a paying guest, but of those who welcome a wanderer and try to make him a home. And so, in a dark-panelled little parlour, with a sedate-ticking clock, I sit while the sounds of life grow fainter and rarer in the little street.

THE CROSSFOXES INN,
BOURTON-ON-THE-WOLD,
April 16, 1904.

DEAR HERBERT,—I have now been ten days on my travels, but for the last week I have pitched my moving tent at Bourton. Do you shudder with the fear that I am going to give you pages of description of scenery? It is not a SHUDDER with me when I get a landscape-letter; it is merely that leaden dulness which falls upon the spirit when it is confronted with statements which produce no impression upon the mind. I always, for instance, skip the letters of travel which appear about the third chapter of great biographies, when the young gentleman goes for the Grand Tour after taking his degree.

But imagine this: a great, rich, wooded, watered plain; on the far horizon the shadowy forms of hills; behind you, gently rising heights, with dingles and folds full of copsewood, rising to soft green downs. There, on the skirts of the upland, above the plain, below the hill, sits the little village, with a stately Perpendicular church tower. The village itself of stone houses, no two alike, all with character; gabled, mullioned, weathered to a delicate ochre—some standing back, some on the street. Intermingled with these are fine Georgian houses, with great pilasters, all of stone too; in the centre of the street a wall, with two tall gate-posts, crowned with stone balls; a short lime avenue leads to a stately, gabled manor-house, which you can see through great iron gates. The whole scene incredibly romantic, exquisitely beautiful.

My favourite walk is this. I leave the little town by a road which winds along the base of the hill. I pass round a shoulder, wooded and covered to the base with tangled thickets, where the birds sing shrilly. I turn up to the left into a kind of "combe." At the very farthest end of the little valley, at the base of the steeper slopes but now high above the plain, stands an ancient church among yews. On one side of it is a long, low-fronted, irregular manor-house, with a formal garden in front, approached by a little arched gate-house which stands on the road; on the other side of the church, and below it, a no less ancient rectory, with a large Perpendicular window, anciently a chapel, in the gable. In the warm, sheltered air the laurels grow luxuriantly; a bickering stream, running in a deep channel, makes a delicate music of its own; a little farther on stands a farm, with barn and byre; in the midst of the buildings is a high, stone-tiled dovecote. The roo-hooing of the pigeons fills the whole place with a slumberous sound. I wind up the hill by a little path, now among thickets, now crossing a tilted pasture. I emerge on the top of a down; in front of me lie the long slopes of the wold, with that purity and tranquillity of outline which only down-land possesses. Here on a spur stands a grass-grown camp, with ancient thorn-trees growing in it. Turning round, the great plain runs for miles, with here and there a glint of water, where the slow-moving Avon wanders. Hamlets, roads, towers lie out like a map at my feet—all wearing that secluded, peaceful air which tempts me to think that life would be easy and happy if it could only be lived among those quiet fields, with the golden light and lengthening shadows.

I find myself wondering in these quiet hours—I walk alone as a rule—what this haunting, incommunicable sense of beauty is. Is it a mere matter of temperament, of inner happiness, of physical well-being; or has it an absolute existence? It comes and goes like the wind. Some days one is acutely, almost painfully, alive to it—painfully, because it makes such constant and insistent demands upon one's attention. Some days, again, it is almost unheeded, and one passes through it blind and indifferent. It is an expression, I cannot help feeling, of the very mind of God; and yet the ancient earthwork in which I stand, bears witness to the fact that in far-off days men lived in danger and anxiety, fighting and striving for bare existence. We have established by law and custom a certain personal security nowadays; is our sense of beauty born of that security? I cannot help wondering whether the old warriors who built this place cared at all for the beauty of the earth; and yet over it all hangs the gentle sadness of all sweet things that have an end. All those warriors are dust; the boys and girls who wandered a century ago where I wander to-day, they are at rest too in the little churchyard that lies at my feet; and my heart goes out to all who have loved and suffered, and to those who shall hereafter love and suffer here. An idle sympathy, perhaps, but none the less strong and real.

But now for a little human experience that befell me here. I found the other day, not far from the church, an old artist sketching. A refined, sad-looking old fellow, sunburned and active, with white hair and pointed beard, and a certain pathetic attempt, of a faded kind, to dress for his part—low collar, a red tie, rough shooting-jacket, and so forth. He seemed in a sociable mood, and I sate down beside him. How it came about I hardly know, but he was soon telling me the story of his life. He was the tenant, I found, of the old manor-house, which he held at a ridiculous rent, and he had lived here nearly forty years. He had found the place as a young man, wandering about in search of the picturesque. I gathered that he had bright dreams and wide ambitions. He had a small independence, and he had meant to paint great pictures and make a name for himself. He had married; his wife was long dead, his children out in the world, and he was living on alone, painting the same pictures, bought, so far as I could make out, mostly by American visitors. His drawing was old-fashioned and deeply mannerised. He was painting not what was there, but some old and faded conception of his own as to what it was like—missing, I think, half the beauty of the place. He seemed horribly desolate. I tried, for his consolation and my own, to draw out a picture of the beautiful refined life he led; and the old fellow began to wear a certain jaunty air of dignity and distinction, which would have amused me if it had not made me feel inclined to cry. But he soon fell back into what is, I suppose, a habitual melancholy. "Ah, if you had known what my dreams were!" he said once. He went on to say that he now wished that he had taken up some simple and straightforward profession, had made money, and had his grandchildren about him. "I am more ghost than man," he said, shaking his dejected head.

I despair of expressing to you the profound pathos that seemed to me to surround this old despondent creature, with his broken dreams and his regretful memories. Where was the mistake he made? I suppose that he over-estimated his powers; but it was a generous mistake after all; and he has had to bear the slow sad disillusionment, the crushing burden of futility. He set out to win glory, and he is a forgotten, shabby, irresolute figure, subsisting on the charity of wealthy visitors! And yet he seems to have missed happiness by so little. To live as he does might be a serene and beautiful thing. If such a man had large reserves of hope and tenderness and patience; if he could but be content with the tranquil beauty of the wholesome earth, spread so richly before his eyes, it would be a life to be envied.

It has been a gentle lesson to me, that one must resolutely practise one's heart and spirit for the closing hours. In the case of successful men, as they grow older, it often strikes me with a sense of pain how passionately they cling to their ambitions and activities. How many people there are who work too long, and try to prolong the energies of morning into the afternoon, and the toil of afternoon into the peace of evening. I earnestly desire to grow old gracefully; to know when to stop, when to slip into a wise and kindly passivity, with sympathy for those who are in the forefront of the race. And yet if one does not practise wonder and receptivity and hope, one cannot expect them to come suddenly and swiftly to one's call. There comes a day when a man ought to be able to see that his best work is behind him, that his active influence is on the wane, that he is losing his hold on the machine. There ought to come a patient, beautiful, and kindly dignity, a love of young things and fresh flowers; not an envious and regretful unhappiness at the loss of the eager life and its brisk sensations, which betrays itself too often in a trickle of exaggerated reminiscences, a "weary, day-long chirping."

This is a harder task, I suppose, for an old bachelor than for a father of children. I have sometimes felt that adoption, with all its risks, of some young creature that you can call your own, would be a solution for many loveless lives, because it would stir them out of the comfortable selfishness that is the bane of the barren heart.

Of course, a schoolmaster suffers from this less than most professional men; but, even so, it is melancholy to reflect how the boys one has cared for, and tried to help, drift out of one's sight and ken. I have no touch of the feeling which they say was characteristic of Jowett—and indeed is amply evidenced by his correspondence—that once a man's tutor he was always his tutor, even though his pupil became grey-headed and a grandfather. One must do the best for the boys and look for no gratitude; it often comes, indeed, in rich measure, but the schoolmaster who craves for it is lost.

Well, it is time to stop. I sit in a little, low raftered parlour of the old inn; the fire in the big hearth flickers into ash, and my candles flare to their sockets. I leave the place to-morrow; and such is the instinct for permanence in the human mind, that I feel depressed and melancholy, as though I were leaving home.—Ever your affectionate,

T. B.

THE BLUE BOAR,
STANTON HARDWICK,
April 21, 1904.

DEAR HERBERT,—I have made a pilgrimage to Stratford-on-Avon. I now feel overwhelmed with shame to reflect that, though my chief preoccupations apart from my profession have been literary, I have never visited the sacred place before. For an Englishman who cares for literature not to have been to Stratford-on-Avon is as gross a neglect as for an Englishman who has any sense of patriotism not to have visited Westminster Abbey.

And now that I have been there and returned, and have leisure to think it all over, I feel that I have been standing on the threshold of a mystery. Who, when all is said and done, was this extraordinary man? What were his thoughts, his aims, his views of himself and of the world? If Shakespeare was Shakespeare, he seems, to speak frankly, to have had a humanity distinct and apart from his genius. Here we have the son of a busy, quarrelsome, enterprising tradesman—who eventually indeed came to grief in trade—of a yeoman stock, and bearing a common name. His mother could not write her own signature. Of his youth we hear little that is not disreputable. He married under unpleasant circumstances, after an entanglement which took place at a very early age; he was addicted to poaching, or, at all events, to the illegal pursuit of other people's game. Then he drifts up to London and joins a theatrical company—then a rascally kind of trade—deserting his wife and family. His life in London is full of secrets. He is a man of mysterious passions and dangerous friendships. He writes plays of incomparable depth and breadth, touching every chord of humour, tragedy and pathos; certain rather elaborate poems of a precieux type, and strange sonnets, revealing a singular poignancy of unconventional feelings. But here, again, it is difficult to conceive that the writer of the Sonnets, who touched life so intensely at one feverish point, should have had the amazing detachment and complexity of mind and soul that the plays reveal. The notices of his talk and character are few and unenlightening, and testify to a certain easy brilliance of wit, but no more. Before he is thirty he is spoken of as both "upright" and "facetious"—a singular combination.

Then he suddenly appears in another aspect; at the age of thirty-two he is a successful, well-to-do man. And then his ambition, if he had any, seems to shift its centre, and he appears to be only bent upon restoring the fortunes of his family, and attaining a solid municipal position. He buys the biggest house in his native place; from the proceeds of his writings, his professional income as an actor, and from his share in the playhouse of which he is part owner, he purchases lands and houses, he engages in lawsuits, he concerns himself with grants of arms. Still the flood of stupendous literature flows out; he seems to be under a contract to produce plays, for which he receives the magnificent sum of L10 (L100 of our money). He writes easily and never corrects. He seems to set no store on his writings, which stream from him like light from the sun. He adapts, collaborates, and has no idea of what would be called a high vocation.

At forty-seven it all ceases; he writes no more, but lives prosperously in his native town, with occasional visits to London. At fifty-two his health fails. He makes business-like arrangements in the event of death, and faces the darkness of the long sleep like any other good citizen.

Who can co-ordinate or reconcile these things? Who can conceive the likeness of the man, who steps in this light-hearted, simple way on to the very highest platform of literature—so lofty and unattainable a place he takes without striving, without arrogance, a throne among the thrones where Homer, Virgil, and Dante sit? And yet his mind is set, not on these things, but on acres and messuages, tithes and investments. He seems not only devoid of personal vanity, but even of that high and solemn pride which made Keats say, with faltering lips, that he believed he would be among the English poets after his death.

I came through the pleasant water-meadows and entered the streets of the busy town. Everything, from bank to eating-shop, bears the name of Shakespeare; and one cannot resist the thought that such local and homely renown would have been more to our simple hero's taste than the laurel and the throne. I groaned in spirit over the monstrous playhouse, with its pretentious Teutonic air; I walked through the churchyard, vocal with building rooks, and came to the noble church, full of the evidences of wealth and worship and honour. I do not like to confess the breathless awe with which I drew near to the chancel and gazed on the stone that, nameless, with its rude rhyme, covers the sacred dust. I cannot say what my thoughts were, but I was lost in a formless, unuttered prayer of true abasement before the venerable relics of the highest achievements of the human spirit. There beneath my feet slept the dust of the brain that conceived Hamlet and Macbeth, and the hand that had traced the Sonnets, and the eye that had plumbed the depths of life. That was a solemn moment, and I do not think I ever experienced so deep a thrill of speechless awe. I could not tear myself away; I could only wonder and desire.

Presently, by the kind offices of a pleasant simple verger, I did more. I mounted on some steps he brought, and looked face to face at the bust in the monument.

I cannot share in the feelings of those who would consider it formal or perfunctory. There was the high-domed forehead, like that of Pericles and Walter Scott; there were the steady eyes, the clear-cut nose; and as for the lips—I never for an instant doubted the truth of what I saw—I am as certain as I can be that they are the lips of a corpse, drawn up in the stiff tension of death, showing the teeth below. I am absolutely convinced that here we get as near to the man as we can get, and that the head is taken from a death-mask. What injures the dignity and beauty of the face is the plumpness of the chin that testifies to the burgher prosperity, the comfortable life, the unexercised brain of the later days. I saw afterwards the various portraits; I suppose it is a matter of evidence, but nothing convinced me of truth, not even the bilious, dilapidated, dyspeptic, white face of the folio engraving, with the horrible hydrocephalous development of skull. That is a caricature only. The others seem mere fancies.

Then I saw patiently the other relics, the foundations of New Place, the schoolhouse—but all without emotion, except a deep sense of shame that the only records allowed to stand in the long, low-latticed room in which the boy Shakespeare probably saw a play first acted, are boards recording the names of school football and cricket teams. The ineptitude of such a proceeding, the hideous insistence of the athletic craze of England, drew from me a despairing smile; but I think that Shakespeare himself would have viewed it with tolerance and even amusement.

But most of these relics, like Anne Hathaway's Cottage, are restored out of all interest, and only testify to the silly and frivolous demands of trippers.

But, my dear Herbert, the treasure is mine. Feeble as the confession is, I do not think I ever realised before the humanity of Shakespeare. He seemed to me before to sit remote, enshrined aloof, the man who could tell all the secrets of humanity that could be told, and whose veriest hints still seem to open doors into mysteries both high and sweet and terrible. But now I feel as if I had been near him, had been able to love what I had only admired.

I feel somehow that it extends the kingdom of humanity to have realised Shakespeare; and yet I am baffled. But I seem to trace in the later and what some would call the commonplace features of the man's life, a desire to live and be; to taste life itself, not merely to write of what life seemed to be, and of what lay behind it. I am sure that some such allegory was in his mind when he wrote of Prospero, who so willingly gave up the isle full of noises, the power over the dreaming, sexless spirits of air and wood, to go back to his tiresome dukedom, and his petty court, and all the dull chatter and business of life. I am sure that Shakespeare thought of his art as an Ariel—that dainty, delicate spirit, out of the reach of love and desire, that slept in cowslip-bells and chased the flying summer on the bat's back, and that yet had such power to delude and bemuse the human spirit. After all, Ariel could not come near the more divine inheritance of the human heart, sorrow and crying, love and hate. Ariel was but a merry child, lost in passionless delights, yearning to be free, to escape; and Prospero felt, and Shakespeare felt, that life, with all its stains and dreariness and disease and darkness, was something better and truer than the fragrant dusk of the copse, and the soulless laughter of the summer sea. Ariel could sing the heartless, exquisite song of the sea-change that could clothe the bones and eyes of the doomed king; but Prospero could see a fairer change in the eyes and heart of his lonely darling.

And I am glad that even so Shakespeare could be silent, and buy and sell, and go in and out among his fellow-townsmen, and make merry. That is better than to sit arid and prosperous, when the brain stiffens with stupor, and the hand has lost its cunning, and to read old newspaper-cuttings, and long for adequate recognition. God give me and all uneasy natures grace to know when to hold our tongues; and to take the days that remain with patience and wonder and tenderness; not making haste to depart, but yet not fearing the shadow out of which we come and into which we must go; to live wisely and bravely and sweetly, and to close our eyes in faith, with a happy sigh, like a child after a long summer day of life and delight.— Ever yours,

T. B.

THE BLUE BOAR,
STANTON HARDWICK,
April 25, 1904.

DEAR HERBERT,—Since I last wrote I have been making pious pilgrimages to some of the great churches hereabouts: to Gloucester, Worcester, Tewkesbury, Malvern, Pershore. It does me good to see these great poems in stone, beautiful in their first conception, and infinitely more beautiful from the mellowing influences of age, and from the human tradition that is woven into them and through them. There are few greater pleasures than to make one's way into a Cathedral city, with the grey towers visible for miles across the plain, rising high above the house roofs and the smoke. At first one is in the quiet country; then the roads begin to have a suburban air—new cottages rise by the wayside, comfortable houses, among shrubberies and plantations. Then the street begins; the houses grow taller and closer, and one has a glimpse of some stately Georgian front, with pediment and cornice; perhaps there is a cluster of factories, high, rattling buildings overtopped by a tall chimney, with dusty, mysterious gear, of which one cannot guess the purport, travelling upwards into some tall, blank orifice. Then suddenly one is in the Close, with trees and flowers and green grass, with quaint Prebendal houses of every style and date, breathing peace and prosperity. A genial parson or two pace gravely about; and above you soars the huge church, with pinnacle and parapet, the jackdaws cheerily hallooing from the lofty ledges. You are a little weary of air and sun; you push open the great door, and you are in the cool, dark nave with its holy smell; you sit for a little and let the spirit of the place creep into your mind; you walk hither and thither, read the epitaphs, mourn with the bereaved, give thanks for the record of long happy lives, and glow with mingled pain and admiration for some young life nobly laid down. The monuments of soldiers, the sight of dusty banners moving faintly in the slow-stirring air, always move me inexpressibly; the stir and fury of war setting hither, like a quiet tide, to find its last abiding-place. Then there is the choir to visit. I do not really like the fashion which now generally prevails of paying a small sum, writing your name in a book, and being handed over to the guidance of some verger, a pompous foolish person, who has learnt his lesson, delivers it like a machine, and is put out by any casual question. I do not want to be lectured; I want to wander about, ask a question if I desire it, and just have pointed out to me anything of which the interest is not patent and obvious. The tombs of old knights, the chantries of silent abbots and bishops, are all very affecting; they stand for so much hope and love and recollection. Then sometimes one has a glow at seeing some ancient and famous piece of history presented to one's gaze. The figure of the grim Saxon king, with his archaic beard and shaven upper-lip, for all the world like some Calvinistic tradesman; or Edward the Second, with his weak, handsome face and curly locks; or the mailed statue of Robert of Normandy, with scarlet surcoat, starting up like a warrior suddenly aroused. Such tombs send a strange thrill through one, a thrill of wonder and pity and awe. What of them now? Sleepest thou, son of Atreus? Dost thou sleep, and dream perchance of love and war, of the little life that seemed so long, and over which the slow waves of time have flowed? Little by little, in the holy walls, so charged with faith and tenderness and wistful love, the pathetic vision of mortality creeps across the mind, and one loses oneself in a dream of wonder at the brief days so full of life, the record left for after time, and the silence of the grave.

Then, when I have drunk my fill of sweet sights, I love to sit silent, while the great bell hums in the roof, and gathering footsteps of young and old patter through the echoing aisles. There is a hush of expectation. A few quiet worshippers assemble; the western light grows low, and lights spring to life, one after another, in the misty choir. Then murmurs a voice, an Amen rises in full concord, and as it dies away the slumberous thunder of a pedal note rolls on the air; the casements whirr, the organ speaks. That fills, as it were, to the brim, as with some sweet and fragrant potion, the cup of beauty; and the dreaming, inquiring spirit sinks content into the flowing, the aspiring tide, satisfied as with some heavenly answer to its sad questionings. Then the stately pomp moves slowly to its place—so familiar, perhaps trivial an act to those who perform it, so grave and beautiful a thing to those who see it. The holy service proceeds with a sense of exquisite deliberation, leading one, as by a ladder, through the ancient ways, up to the message of to-day. Through psalm and canticle and anthem the solemnity passes on; and perhaps some single slender voice, some boyish treble, unconscious of its beauty and pathos, thrown into relief, like a fountain springing among dark rocks, by the slow thunders of the organ, comes to assure the heart that it can rest, if but for a moment, upon a deep and inner peace, can be gently rocked, as it were, in a moving boat, between the sky and translucent sea. Then falls the rich monotone of prayer; and the organ wakes again for one last message, pouring a flood of melody from its golden throats, and dying away by soft gradations into the melodious bourdon of its close.

Does this seem to you very unreal and fantastic? I do not know; it is very real to me. Sometimes, in dreary working hours, my spirit languishes under an almost physical thirst for such sweetness of sound and sight. I cannot believe that it is other than a pure and holy pleasure, because in such hours the spirit soars into a region in which low and evil thoughts, ugly desires, and spiteful ambitions, die, like poisonous flowers in a clear and wholesome air. I do not say that it inspires one with high and fierce resolution, that it fits one for battling with the troublesome world; but it is more like the green pastures and waters of comfort; it is pleasure in which there is no touch of sensual appetite or petty desire; it is a kind of heavenly peace in which the spirit floats in a passionate longing for what is beautiful and pure. It is not that I would live my life in such reveries; even while the soft sound dies away, the calling of harsher voices makes itself heard in the mind. But it refreshes, it calms, it pacifies; it tells the heart that there is a peace into which it is possible to enter, and where it may rest for a little and fold its weary wings.

Yet even as I write, as the gentle mood lapses and fades, I find myself beset with uneasy and bewildering thoughts about the whole. What was the power that raised these great places as so essential and vital a part of life? We have lost it now, whatever it was. Churches like these were then an obvious necessity; kings and princes vied with each other in raising them, and no one questioned their utility. They are now a mere luxury for ecclesiastically minded persons, built by slow accretion, and not by some huge single gift, to please the pride of a county or a city; and this in days when England is a thousandfold richer than she was. They are no longer a part of the essence of life; life has flowed away from their portals, and left them a beautiful shadow, a venerable monument, a fragrant sentiment. No doubt it was largely superstition that constructed them, a kind of insurance paid for heavenly security. No one now seriously thinks that to endow a college of priests to perform services would affect his spiritual prospects in the life to come. The Church itself does not countenance the idea. Moreover, there is little demand in the world at large for the kind of beauty which they can and do minister to such as myself. The pleasure for which people spend money nowadays has to have a stirring, exciting, physical element in it to be acceptable. If it were otherwise, then our cathedrals could take their place in the life of the nation; but they are out of touch with railways, and newspapers, and the furious pursuit of athletics. They are on the side of peace and delicate impressions and quiet emotions. I wish it were not so; but it would be faithless to believe that we are not in the hand of God still, and that our restless energies develop against His will.

And then there falls a darker, more bewildering thought. Suppose that one could bring one of the rough Galilean fishermen who sowed the seed of the faith, into a place like this, and say to him, "This is the fruit of your teaching; you, whose Master never spoke a word of art or music, who taught poverty and simplicity, bareness of life, and an unclouded heart, you are honoured here; these towers and bells are called after your names; you stand in gorgeous robes in these storied windows." Would they not think and say that it was all a terrible mistake? would they not say that the desire of the world, the lust of the eye and ear, had laid subtle and gentle hands on a stern and rugged creed, and bade it serve and be bound?

"Thy nakedness involves thy Spouse
In the soft sanguine stuff she wears."

So says an eager and vehement poet, apostrophising the tortured limbs, the drooping eye of the Crucified Lord; and is it true that these stately and solemn houses, these sweet strains of unearthly music, serve His purpose and will? Nay, is it not rather true that the serpent is here again aping the mildness of the dove, and using all the delicate, luxurious accessories of life to blind us to the truth?

I do not know; it leaves me in a sad and bewildered conflict of spirit. And yet I somehow feel that God is in these places, and that, if only the heart is pure and the will strong, such influences can minister to the growth of the meek and loving spirit.—Ever yours,

T. B.

I don't know what has happened to your letters. Perhaps you have not been able to write? I go back to work to-morrow.

UPTON,
May 2, 1904.

MY DEAR HERBERT,—My holidays are over, and I am back at work again. I have got your delightful letter; it was silly to be anxious....

To-day I was bicycling; I was horribly preoccupied, as, alas, I often am, with my own plans and thoughts. I was worrying myself about my work, fretting about the thousand little problems that beset a schoolmaster, trying to think out a chapter of a book which I am endeavouring to write, my mind beating and throbbing like a feverish pulse. I kept telling myself that the copses were beautiful, that the flowers were enchanting, that the long line of distant hills seen across the wooded valleys and the purple plain were ravishingly tranquil and serene; but it was of no use; my mind ran like a mill-race, a stream of thoughts jostling and hurrying on, in spite of my efforts to shut the sluice.

Suddenly I turned a corner by a little wood, and found myself looking over into the garden of a small, picturesque cottage, which has been smartened up lately, and has become, I suppose, the country retreat of some well-to-do people. It was a pretty garden; a gentle slope of grass, borders full of flowers, and an orchard behind, whitening into bloom, with a little pool in the shady heart of it. On the lawn were three people, obviously and delightfully idle; an elderly man sate in a chair, smiling, smoking, reading a paper. The other two, a younger man and a young woman, were walking side by side, their heads close together, laughing quietly at some gentle jest. A perambulator stood by the porch. Both the men looked like prosperous professional people, clean-shaven, healthy, and contented. I inferred, for no particular reason, that the young pair were man and wife, lately married, and that the elder man was the father-in-law. I had this passing glimpse, no more, of an interior; and then I was riding among the spring woods again.

Of course it was only an impression, but this happy, sunshiny scene, so suddenly opened to my gaze, so suddenly closed again, was like a parable. I felt as if I should have liked to stop, to take off my hat, and thank my unknown friends for making so simple, pleasant, and sweet a picture. I dare say they were as preoccupied in professional matters, as careful and troubled as myself, if I had known more about them. But in that moment they were finding leisure simply to taste and enjoy the wholesome savours of life, and were neither looking backward in regret nor forward in anticipation. I dare say the jokes that amused them were mild enough, and that I should have found their conversation tedious and tiresome if I had been made one of the party. But they were symbolical; they stood for me, and will stand, as a type of what we ought to aim at more; and that is simply LIVING. It is a lesson which you yourself are no doubt learning in your fragrant, shady garden. You have no need to make money, and your only business is to get better. But for myself, I know that I work and think and hope and fear too much, and that in my restless pursuit of a hundred aims and ambitions and dreams and fancies, I am constantly in danger of hardly living at all, but of simply racing on, like a man intoxicated with affairs, without leisure for strolling, for sitting, for talking, for watching the sky and the earth, smelling the scents of flowers, noting the funny ways of animals, playing with children, eating and drinking. Yet this is our true heritage, and this is what it means to be a man; and, after all, one has (for all one knows) but a single life, and that a short one. It is at such moments as these that I wake as from a dream, and think how fast my life flows on, and how very little conscious of its essence I am. My head is full from morning to night of everything except living. For a busy man this is, of course, to a certain extent inevitable. But where I am at fault is in not relapsing at intervals into a wise and patient passivity, and sitting serenely on the shore of the sea of life, playing with pebbles, seeing the waves fall and the ships go by, and wondering at the strange things cast up by the waves, and the sharp briny savours of the air. Why do I not do this? Because, to continue my confession, it bores me. I must, it seems, be always in a fuss; be always hauling myself painfully on to some petty ambition or some shadowy object that I have in view; and the moment I have reached it, I must fix upon another, and begin the process over again. It is this lust for doing something tangible, for sitting down quickly and writing fifty, for having some definite result to show, which is the ruin of me and many others. After all, when it is done, what worth has it? I am not a particularly successful man, and I can't delude myself into thinking that my work has any very supreme value. And meanwhile all the real experiences of life pass me by. I have never, God forgive me, had time to be in love! That is a pitiful confession.

Sometimes one comes across a person with none of these uneasy ambitions, with whom living is a fine art; then one realises what a much more beautiful creation it is than books and pictures. It is a kind of sweet and solemn music. Such a man or woman has time to read, to talk, to write letters, to pay calls, to walk about the farm, to go and sit with tiresome people, to spend long hours with children, to sit in the open air, to keep poultry, to talk to servants, to go to church, to remember what his or her relations are doing, to enjoy garden parties and balls, to like to see young people enjoying themselves, to hear confessions, to do other people's business, to be a welcome presence everywhere, and to leave a fragrant memory, watered with sweet tears. That is to live. And such lives, one is tempted to think, were more possible, more numerous, a hundred years ago. But now one expects too much, and depends too much on exciting pleasures, whether of work or play. Well, my three persons in a garden must be a lesson to me; and, whatever may really happen to them, in my mind they shall walk for ever between the apple-trees and the daffodils, looking lovingly at each other, while the elder man shall smile as he reads in the Chronicle of Heaven, which does not grow old.—Ever yours,

T. B.

UPTON,
May 9, 1904.

MY DEAR HERBERT,—I am going back to the subject of ambition—do you mind?

Yesterday in chapel one of my colleagues preached rather a fine sermon on Activity. The difficulty under which he laboured is a common one in sermons; it is simply this—How far is a Christian teacher justified in recommending ambition to Christian hearers? I think that, if one reads the Gospel, it is clear that ambition is not a Christian motive. The root of the teaching of Christ seems to me to be that one should have or acquire a passion for virtue; love it for its beauty, as an artist loves beauty of form or colour; and the simplicity which is to be the distinguishing mark of a Christian seems to me to be inconsistent with personal ambition. I do not see that there is any hint of a Christian being allowed to wish to do, what is called in domestic language "bettering" himself. The idea rather is that the all-wise and all-loving Father puts a man into the world where he intends him to be; and that a man is to find his highest pleasure in trying to serve the Father's will, with a heart full of love for all living things. A rich man is to disembarrass himself of his riches, or at least be sure that they are no hindrance to him; a poor man is not to attempt to win them. Of course it may be possible that the original Christians were intended to take a special line while the faith was leavening the world, and that a different economy was to prevail when society had been Christianised. This is a point of view which can be subtly defended, but I think it is hard to find any justification for it in the Gospel. Ambition practically means that, if one is to shoulder to the front, one must push other people out of the way; one must fight for one's own hand. To succeed at no one's expense is only possible to people of very high character and genius.

But it is difficult to see what motive to set before boys in the matter; the ideas of fame and glory, the hope of getting what all desire and what all cannot have, are deeply rooted in the childish mind. Moreover, we encourage ambition so frankly, both in work and play, that it is difficult to ascend the school pulpit and take quite a different line. To tell boys that they must simply do their best for the sake of doing their best, without any thought of the rewards of success—it is a very fine ideal, but is it a practical one? If we gave prizes to the stupid boys who work without hope of success, and if we gave colours to the boys who played games hard without attaining competence in them, we might then dare to speak of the rewards of virtue. But boys despise unsuccessful conscientiousness, and all the rewards we distribute are given to aptitude. Some preachers think they get out of the difficulty by pointing to examples of lives that battled nobly and unsuccessfully against difficulties; but the point always is the ultimate recognition. The question is not whether we can provide a motive for the unsuccessful; but whether we ought not to discourage ambition in every form? Yet it is the highest motive power in the case of most generous and active-minded boys.

In the course of the sermon the preacher quoted some lines of Omar Khayyam in order to illustrate the shamefulness of the indolent life. That is a very dangerous thing to do. The lovely stanzas, sweet as honey, flowed out upon the air in all their stately charm. The old sinner stole my heart away with his gentle, seductive, Epicurean grace. I am afraid that I felt like Paolo as he sate beside Francesca. I heard no more of the sermon that day; I repeated to myself many of the incomparable quatrains, and felt the poem to be the most beautiful presentment of pure Agnosticism that has ever been given to the world. The worst of it is that the delicate traitor makes it so beautiful that one does not feel the shame and the futility of it.

This evening I have been reading the new life of FitzGerald, so you may guess what was the result of the sermon for me. It is not a wholly pleasing book, but it is an interesting one; it gives a better picture of the man than any other book or article, simply by the great minuteness with which it enters into details. And now I find myself confronted by the problem in another shape. Was FitzGerald's life an unworthy one? He had great literary ambitions, but he made nothing of them. He lived a very pure, innocent, secluded life, delighting in nature and in the company of simple people; loving his friends with a passion that reminds one of Newman; doing endless little kindnesses to all who came within his circle; and tenderly loved by several great-hearted men of genius. He felt himself that he was to blame; he urged others to the activities which he could not practise. And yet the results of his life are such as many other more busy, more conscientious men have not achieved. He has left a large body of good literary work, and one immortal poem of incomparable beauty. He also left, quite unconsciously, I believe, many of the most beautiful, tender, humorous, wise letters in the English tongue; and I find myself wondering whether all this could have been brought to pass in any other way.

Yet I could not conscientiously advise any one to take FitzGerald's life as a model It was shabby, undecided, futile; he did many silly, almost fatuous things; he was deplorably idle and unstrung. At the same time a terrible suspicion creeps upon me that many busy men are living worse lives. I don't mean men who give themselves to activities, however dusty, which affect other people. I will grant at once that doctors, teachers, clergymen, philanthropists, even Members of Parliament are justified in their lives; then, too, men who do the necessary work of the world—farmers, labourers, workmen, fishermen, are justifiable. But business men who make fortunes for their children; lawyers, artists, writers, who work for money and for praise—are these after all so much nobler than our indolent friend? To begin with, FitzGerald's life was one of extraordinary simplicity. He lived on almost nothing, he had no luxuries; he was like a lily of the field. If he had been a merely selfish man it would have been different; but he loved his fellow-men deeply and tenderly, and he showered unobtrusive kindness on all round him.

I find it very hard to make up my mind; it is true that the fabric of the world would fall to pieces if we were all FitzGeralds. But so, too, as has often been pointed out, would it fall to pieces if we all lived literally on the lines of the Sermon on the Mount. Activities are for many people a purely selfish thing, to fill the time because they are otherwise bored; and it is hard to see why a man who can fill his life with less strenuous pleasures, books, music, strolling, talking, should not be allowed to do so.

Solve me the riddle, if you can! The simplicity of the Gospel seems to me to be inconsistent with the Expansion of England; and I dare not say off-hand that the latter is the finer ideal.—Ever yours,

T. B.

UPTON,
May 15, 1904.

MY DEAR HERBERT,—You ask if I have read anything lately? Well, I have been reading Stalky & Co. with pain, and, I hope, profit. It is an amazing book; the cleverness, the freshness, the incredible originality of it all; the careless ease with which scene after scene is touched off and a picture brought before one at a glance, simply astounds me, and leaves me gasping. But I don't want now to discourse about the literary merits of the book, great as they are. I want to relieve my mind of the thoughts that disquiet me. I think, to start with, it is not a fair picture of school life at all. If it is really reminiscent—and the life-likeness and verisimilitude of the book is undeniable—the school must have been a very peculiar one. In the first place, the interest is concentrated upon a group of very unusual boys. The Firm of Stalky is, I humbly thank God, a combination of boys of a rare species. The other figures of boys in the book form a mere background, and the deeds of the central heroes are depicted like the deeds of the warriors of the Iliad. They dart about, slashing and hewing, while the rank and file run hither and thither like sheep, their only use being in the numerical tale of heads that they can afford to the flashing blades of the protagonists; and even so the chief figures, realistic though they are, remind me not so much of spirited pictures as of Gillray's caricatures. They are highly coloured, fantastic, horribly human and yet, somehow, grotesque. Everything is elongated, widened, magnified, exaggerated. The difficulty is, to my mind, to imagine boys so lawless, so unbridled, so fond at intervals of low delights, who are yet so obviously wholesome-minded and manly. I can only humbly say that it is my belief, confirmed by experience, that boys of so unconventional and daring a type would not be content without dipping into darker pleasures. But Kipling is a great magician, and, in reading the book, one can thankfully believe that in this case it was not so; just as one can also believe that, in this particular case, the boys were as mature and shrewd, and of as complete and trenchant a wit as they appear. My own experience here again is that no boys could keep so easily on so high a level of originality and sagacity. The chief characteristic of all the boys I have ever known is that they are so fitful, so unfinished. A clever boy will say incredibly acute things, but among a dreary tract of wonderfully silly ones. The most original boys will have long lapses into conventionality, but the heroes of Kipling's book are never conventional, never ordinary; and then there is an absence of restfulness which is one of the greatest merits of Tom Brown.

But what has made the book to me into a kind of Lenten manual is the presentation of the masters. Here I see, portrayed with remorseless fidelity, the faults and foibles of my own class; and I am sorry to say that I feel deliberately, on closing the book, that schoolmastering must be a dingy trade. My better self cries out against this conclusion, and tries feebly to say that it is one of the noblest of professions; and then I think of King and Prout, and all my highest aspirations die away at the thought that I may be even as these.

I suppose that Kipling would reply that he has done full justice to the profession by giving us the figures of the Headmaster and the Chaplain. The Headmaster is obviously a figure which his creator regards with respect. He is fair-minded, human, generous; it is true that he is enveloped with a strange awe and majesty; he moves in a mysterious way, and acts in a most inconsequent and unexpected manner. But he generally has the best of a situation; and though there is little that is pastoral about him, yet he is obviously a wholesome-minded, manly sort of person, who whips the right person at the right time, and generally scores in the end. But he is a Roman father, at best. He has little compassion and no tenderness; he is acute, brisk, and sensible; but he has (at least to me) neither grace nor wisdom; or, if he has, he keeps them under a polished metallic dish-cover, and only lifts it in private. I do not feel that the Headmaster has any religion, except the religion of all sensible men. In seeming to despise all sentiment, Kipling seems to me to throw aside several beautiful flowers, tied carelessly up in the same bundle. There should be a treasure in the heart of a wise schoolmaster; not to be publicly displayed nor drearily recounted; but at the right moment, and in the right way, he ought to be able to show a boy that there are sacred and beautiful things which rule or ought to rule the heart. If the Head has such a treasure he keeps it at the bank and only visits it in the holidays.

The "Padre" is a very human figure—to me the most attractive in the book; he has some wisdom and tenderness, and his little vanities are very gently touched. But (I daresay I am a very pedantic person) I don't really like his lounging about and smoking in the boys' studies. I think that what he would have called tolerance is rather a deplorable indolence, a desire to be above all things acceptable. He earns his influence by giving his colleagues away, and he seems to me to think more of the honour of the boys than of the honour of the place.

But King and Prout, the two principal masters—it is they who spoil the taste of my food and mingle my drink with ashes. They are, in their way, well-meaning and conscientious men. But is it not possible to love discipline without being a pedant, and to be vigilant without being a sneak? I fear in the back of my heart that Kipling thinks that the trade of a schoolmaster is one which no generous or self-respecting man can adopt. And yet it is a useful and necessary trade; and we should be in a poor way if it came to be regarded as a detestable one. I wish with all my heart that Kipling had used his genius to make our path smoother instead of rougher. The path of the schoolmaster is indeed set round with pitfalls. A man who is an egotist and a bully finds rich pasturage among boys who are bound to listen to him, and over whom he can tyrannise. But, on the other hand, a man who is both brave and sensitive—and there are many such—can learn as well as teach abundance of wholesome lessons, if he comes to his task with some hope and love. King is, of course, a verbose bully; he delights in petty triumphs; he rejoices in making himself felt; he is a cynic as well, a greedy and low-minded man; he takes a disgusting pleasure in detective work; he begins by believing the worst of boys; he is vain, shy, irritable; he is cruel, and likes to see his victim writhe. I have known many schoolmasters and I have never known a Mr. King, except perhaps at a private school. But even King has done me good; he has confirmed me in my belief that more can be done by courtesy and decent amiability than can ever be done by discipline enforced by hard words. He teaches me not to be pompous, and not to hunger and thirst after finding things out. He makes me feel sure that the object of detection is to help boys to be better, and not to have the satisfaction of punishing them.

Prout is a feeble sentimentalist, with a deep belief in phrases. He is a better fellow than King, and is only an intolerable goose. Both the men make me wish to burst upon the scene, when they are grossly mishandling some simple situation; but while I want to kick King, when he is retreating with dignity, my only desire is to explain to Prout as patiently as I can what an ass he is. He is a perfect instance of absolutely ineffective virtue, a plain dish unseasoned with salt.

There are, of course, other characters in the book, each of them grotesque and contemptible in his own way, each of them a notable example of what not to be. But I would pardon this if the book were not so unjust; if Kipling had included in his gathering of masters one kindly, serious gentleman, whose sense of vocation did not make him a prig. And if he were to reply that the Headmaster fulfils these conditions, I would say that the Headmaster is a prig in this one point, that he is so desperately afraid of priggishness. The manly man, to my mind, is the man who does not trouble his head as to whether he is manly or not, not the man who wears clothes too big for him, and heavy boots, treads like an ox, and speaks gruffly; that is a pose, not better or worse than other poses. And what I want in the book is a man of simple and direct character, interested in his work, and not ashamed of his interest; attached to the boys, and not ashamed of seeming to care.

My only consolation is that I have talked to a good many boys who have read the book; they have all been amused, interested, delighted. But they say frankly that the boys are not like any boys they ever knew, and, when I timidly inquire about the masters, they laugh rather sheepishly, and say that they don't know about that.

I am sure that we schoolmasters have many faults; but we are really trying to do better, and, as I said before, I only wish that a man of Kipling's genius had held out to us a helping hand, instead of giving us a push back into the ugly slough of usherdom, out of which many good fellows, my friends and colleagues, have, however feebly, been struggling to emerge.—Ever yours,

T. B.

UPTON,
May 21, 1904.

MY DEAR HERBERT,—I have been wondering since I wrote last whether I could possibly write a school story. I have often desired to try. The thing has hardly ever been well done. Tom Brown remains the best. Dean Farrar's books, vigorous in a sense as they are, are too sentimental. Stalky & Co., as I said in my last letter, in spite of its amazing cleverness of insight, is not typical. Gilkes' books are excellent studies of the subject, but lack unity of theme; Tim is an interesting book, but reflects a rather abnormal point of view; A Day of My Life at Eton is too definitely humorous in conception, though it has great verisimilitude.

In the first place the plot is a difficulty; the incidents of school life do not lend themselves to dramatic situations. Then, too, the trivialities of which school life is so much composed, the minuteness of the details involved, make the subject a singularly complicated one; another great difficulty is to give any idea of the conversations of boys, which are mainly concerned with small concrete facts and incidents, and are lacking in humour and flexibility.

Again, to speak frankly, there is a Rabelaisian plainness of speech on certain subjects, which one must admit to be apt to characterise boys' conversation, which it is impossible to construct or include, and yet the omission of which subtracts considerable reality from the picture. Genius might triumph over all these obstacles, of course, but even a genius would find it very difficult to put himself back into line with the immaturity and narrow views of boys; their credulity, their preoccupations, their conventionality, their inarticulateness—all these qualities are very hard to indicate. Only a boy could formulate these things, and no boy has sufficient ease of expression to do so, or sufficient detachment both to play the part and describe it. A very clever undergraduate, with a gift of language, might write a truthful school-book; but yet the task seems to require a certain mellowness and tolerance which can only be given by experience; and then the very experience would tend to blunt the sharpness of the impressions.

As a rule, in such books, the whole conception of boyhood seems at fault; a boy is generally represented as a generous, heedless, unworldly creature. My experience leads me to think that this is very wide of the mark. Boys are the most inveterate Tories. They love monopoly and privilege, they are deeply subservient, they have little idea of tolerance or justice or fair-play, they are intensely and narrowly ambitious; they have a certain insight into character, but there are some qualities, like vulgarity, which they seem incapable of detecting. They have a great liking for jobs and small indications of power. They are not, as a rule, truthful; they have no compassion for weakness. It is generally supposed that they have a strong sense of liberty, but this is not the case; they are, indeed, tenacious of their rights, or what they suppose to be their rights, but they have little idea of withstanding tyranny, they are incapable of democratic combination, and submit blindly to custom and tradition. Neither do I think them notably affectionate or grateful; everything that is done for them within the limits of a prescribed and habitual system they accept blindly and as a matter of course, while at the same time they are profoundly affected by any civility or sympathy shown them outside the ordinary course of life. I mean that they do not differentiate between a master who takes immense trouble over his work, and discharges his duties with laborious conscientiousness, and a master who saves himself all possible trouble; they are not grateful for labour expended on them, and they do not resent neglect. But a master who asks boys to breakfast, talks politely to them, takes an interest in them in a sociable way, will win a popularity which a laborious and inarticulate man cannot attain to. They are extremely amenable to any indications of personal friendship, while they are blind to the virtues of a master who only studies their best interests. They will work, for instance, with immense vigour for a man who praises and appreciates industry; but a man who grimly insists on hard and conscientious work is looked upon as a person who finds enjoyment in a kind of slave-driving.

Boys are, in fact, profound egoists and profound individualists. Of course there are exceptions to all this; there are boys of deep affection, scrupulous honesty, active interests, keen and far-reaching ambitions; but I am trying to sketch not the exception but the rule.

You will ask what there is left? What there is that makes boys interesting and attractive to deal with? I will tell you. There is, of course, the mere charm of youthfulness and simplicity. And the qualities that I have depicted above are really the superficial qualities, the conventions that boys adopt from the society about them. The nobler qualities of human nature are latent in many boys; but they are for the most part superficially ruled by an intensely strong mauvaise honte, which leads them to live in two worlds, and to keep the inner life very sharply and securely ruled off from the outer. They must be approached tactfully and gently as individuals. It is possible to establish a personal and friendly relation with many boys, so long as they understand that it is a kind of secret understanding, and will not be paraded or traded upon in public. In their inner hearts there are the germs of many high and beautiful things, which tend, unless a boy has some wise and tender older friend—a mother, a father, a sister, even a master—to be gradually obscured under the insistent demands of his outer life. Boys are very diffident about these matters, and require to be encouraged and comforted about them. The danger of public schools, with overworked masters, is that the secret life is apt to get entirely neglected, and then these germs of finer qualities get neither sunshine or rain. Public spirit, responsibility, intellectual interests, unconventional hopes, virtuous dreams—a boy is apt to think that to speak of such things is to incur the reproach of priggishness; but a man who can speak of them naturally and without affectation, who can show that they are his inner life too, and are not allowed to flow in a sickly manner into his outer life, who has a due and wise reserve, can have a very high and simple power for good.

But to express all this in the pages of a book is an almost impossible task; what one wants is to get the outer life briskly and sharply depicted, and to speak of the inner in hints and flashes. Unfortunately, the man who really knows boys is apt to get so penetrated with the pathos, the unrealised momentousness, the sad shipwrecks of boy life that he is not light-hearted enough to depict the outer side of it all, and a book becomes morbid and sentimental. Then, too, to draw a boy correctly would often be to produce a sense of contrast which would almost give a feeling of hypocrisy, because there are boys—and not unfrequently the most interesting—who, if fairly drawn, would appear frivolous, silly, conventional in public, even coarse, who yet might have very fine things behind, though rarely visible. Moreover, the natural, lively, chattering boys, whom it would be a temptation to try and draw, are not really the most interesting. They tend to develop into bores of the first water in later life. But the boy who develops into a fine man is often ungainly, shy, awkward, silent in early life, acutely sensitive, and taking refuge in bluntness or dumbness.

The most striking instances that have come under my own experience, where a boy has really revealed the inside of his mind and spirit, are absolutely incapable of being expressed in words. If I were to write down what boys have said to me, on critical occasions, the record would be laughed at as impossible and unnatural.

So you see that the difficulties are well-nigh insuperable. Narrative would be trivial, conversation affected, motives inexplicable; for, indeed, the crucial difficulty is the absolute unaccountableness of boys' actions and words. A schoolmaster gets to learn that nothing is impossible; a boy of apparently unblemished character will behave suddenly in a manner that makes one despair of human nature, a black sheep will act and speak like an angel of light. The interest is the mystery and the impenetrability of it all; it is so impossible to foresee contingencies or to predict conduct. This impulsiveness, as a rule, diminishes in later life under the influence of maturity and material conditions. But the boy remains insoluble, now a demon, now an angel; and thus the only conclusion is that it is better to take things as they come, and not to attempt to describe the indescribable.—Ever yours,

T. B.

UPTON,
May 28, 1904.

DEAR HERBERT,—I am bursting with news. I am going to tell you a
secret. I have been offered an important Academical post; that is to say, I
received a confidential intimation that I should be elected if I stood. The
whole thing is confidential, so that I must not even tell you what the offer
was. I should have very much liked to talk it over with you, but I had to
make up my mind quickly; there was no time to write, and, moreover, I
feel sure that when I had turned out the pros and cons of my own feelings
for your inspection, you would have decided as I did.

You will say at once that you do not know how I reconciled my refusal
with the cardinal article of my faith, that our path is indicated to us by
Providence, and that we ought to go where we are led. Well, I confess that
I felt this to be a strong reason for accepting. The invitation came to me as
a complete surprise, absolutely unsought, and from a body of electors who
know the kind of man they want and have a large field to choose from;
there was no question of private influence or private friendship. I hardly
know one of the committee; and they took a great deal of trouble in
making inquiries about men.

But, to use a detestable word, there is a strong difference between an
outward call and an inward call. It is not the necessary outcome of a belief
in Providence that one accepts all invitations, and undertakes whatever
one may be asked to do. There is such a thing as temptation; and there is
another kind of summons, sent by God, which seems to come in order that
one may take stock of one's own position and capacities and realise what
one's line ought to be. It is like a passage in a labyrinth which strikes off at
right angles from the passage one is following; the fact that one MAY take
a sudden turn to the left is not necessarily a clear indication that one is
meant to do so. It may be only sent to make one consider the reasons
which induce one to follow the path on which one is embarked.

I had no instantaneous corresponding sense that it was my duty to follow
this call. I was (I will confess it) a little dazzled; but, as soon as that wore
off, I felt an indescribable reluctance to undertake the task, a
consciousness of not being equal to it, a strong sense that I was intended
for other things.

I don't mean to say that there was not much that was attractive about the offer in a superficial way. It meant money, power, position, and consequence—all good things, and good things which I unreservedly like. I am like every one else in that respect; I should like a large house, and a big income, and professional success, and respect and influence as much as any one—more, indeed, than many people.

But I soon saw that this would be a miserable reason for being tempted by the offer, the delight of being called Rabbi. I don't pretend to be high-minded, but even I could see that, unless there was a good deal more than that in my mind, I should be a wretched creature to be influenced by such considerations. These are merely the conveniences; the real point was the work, the power, the possibility of carrying out certain educational reforms which I have very much at heart, and doing something towards raising the general intellectual standard, which I believe to be lower than it need be.

Now, on thinking it out carefully, I came to the conclusion that I was not strong enough for this role. I am no Atlas; I have no deep store of moral courage; I am absurdly sensitive, ill-fitted to cope with unpopularity and disapproval. Bitter, vehement, personal hostility would break my spirit. A fervent Christian might say that one had no right to be faint-hearted, and that strength would be given one; that is perfectly true in certain conditions, and I have often experienced it when some intolerable and inevitable calamity had to be faced. But it is an evil recklessness not to weigh one's own deficiencies. No one would say that a man ignorant of music ought to undertake to play the organ, if the organist failed to appear, believing that power would be given him. Christ Himself warned His disciples against embarking in an enterprise without counting the cost. But here I confess was the darkest point of my dilemma—was it cowardice and indolence to refuse to attempt what competent persons believed I could do? or was it prudent and wise to refuse to attempt what I, knowing my own temperament better, felt I could not attempt successfully?

Now in my present work it is different. I know that my strength is equal to the responsibility; I know that I can do what I undertake. The art of dealing with boys is very different from the art of dealing with men, the capacity for subordinate command is very different from the capacity for supreme command. Of course, it is a truism to say that if a man can obey thoroughly and loyally he can probably command. But then, again, there is a large class of people, to which I believe myself to belong, who are held to be, in the words of Tacitus, Capax imperii, nisi imperasset.

Then, too, I felt that a great task must be taken up in a certain buoyancy and cheerfulness of spirit, not in heaviness and diffidence. There are, of course, instances where a work reluctantly undertaken has been crowned with astonishing success. But one has no business to think that reluctance and diffidence to undertake a great work are a proof that God intends one to do it.

I am quite aware of the danger which a temperament like my own runs, of dealing with such a situation in too complex and subtle a way. That is the hardest thing of all to get rid of, because it is part of the very texture of one's mind. I have tried, however, to see the whole thing in as simple a light as possible, and to ask myself whether acceptance was in any sense a plain duty. If the offer had been a constraining appeal, I should have doubted. But it was made in an easy, complimentary way, as if there was no doubt that I should fall in with it.

Well, I had a very anxious day; but I simply (I may say that to you) prayed that my way might be made clear; and the result was a conviction, which rose like a star and then, as it were, waxed into a sun, that the quest was not for me.

And so I refused; and I am thankful to say that I have had, ever since, the blessed and unalterable conviction that I have done right. Even the conveniences have ceased to appeal to me; they have not even, like the old Adam in the Pilgrim's Progress, pinched hold of me and given me a deadly twitch. Though the picturesque mind of one who, like myself, is very sensitive to "the attributes of awe and majesty," takes a certain peevish pleasure in continuing to depict my unworthy self clothed upon with majesty, and shaking all Olympus with my nod.

But if Olympus had refused to shake, even though I had nodded like a mandarin?

I am sure that I shall not regret it; and I do not even think that my conscience will reproach me; nor do I think that (on this ground alone) I shall be relegated to the dark circle of the Inferno with those who had a great opportunity given them and would not use it.

Please confirm me if you can! Comfort me with apples, as the Song says. I am afraid you will only tell me that it proves that you are right, and that I have no ambition.—Ever yours,

T. B.

UPTON,
June 4, 1904.

DEAR HERBERT,—I have nothing to write about. The summer is come, and with it I enter into purgatory; I am poured out like water, and my heart is like melting wax; I have neither courage nor kindness, except in the early morning or the late evening. I cannot work, and I cannot be lazy. The only consolation I have—and I wish it were a more sustaining one—is that most people like hot weather better.

I will put down for you in laborious prose what if I were an artist I would do in half-a-dozen strokes. There is a big place near here, Rushton Park. I was bicycling with Randall past the lodge, blaming the fair summer, like the fisherman in Theocritus, when he asked if I should like to ride through. The owner, Mr. Payne, is a friend of his, and laid a special injunction on him to go through whenever he liked. We were at once admitted, and in a moment we were in a Paradise. Payne is famed for his gardeners, and I think I never saw a more beautiful place of its kind. The ground undulates very gracefully, and we passed by velvety lawns, huge towering banks of rhododendron all ablaze with flower, exquisite vistas and glades, with a view of far-off hills. It seemed to me to be an enchanted pleasaunce, like the great Palace in The Princess. Now and then we could see the huge facade of the house above us, winking through its sunblinds. There was not a soul to be seen; and this added enormously to the magical charm of the place, as though it were the work of a Genie, not made with hands. We passed a huge fountain dripping into a blue-tiled pool, over a great cockleshell of marble; then took a path which wound into the wood, all a mist of fresh green, and in a moment we were in a long old-fashioned garden, with winding box hedges, and full of bright flowers. To the left, where the garden was bordered by the wood, was set a row of big marble urns, grey with age, on high pedestals, all dripping with flowering creepers. It was very rococo, like an old French picture, but enchanting for all that. To the right was a long, mellow brick wall, under which stood some old marble statues, weather-stained and soft of hue. The steady sun poured down on the sweet, bright place, and the scent of the flowers filled the air with fragrance, while a dove, hidden in some green towering tree, roo-hooed delicately, as though her little heart was filled with an indolent contentment.

The statue that stood nearest us attracted my attention. I cannot conceive what it was meant to represent. It was the figure of an old, bearded man, with a curious brimless hat on his head, and a flowing robe; in his hands he held and fingered some unaccountable object of a nondescript shape; and he had an unpleasant fixed smile, which he seemed to turn on us, as though he knew a secret connected with the garden which he might not reveal, and which if revealed would fill the hearers with a secret horror. I do not think that I have often seen a figure which affected me so disagreeably. He seemed to be saying that within this bright and fragrant place lay some tainted mystery which it were ill to tamper with. It was as though we opened a door out of some stately corridor, and found a strange, beast-like thing running to and fro in a noble room.

Well, I do not know! But it seems to me a type of many things, and I doubt not that the wise-hearted patrician, the former owner, who laid out the garden and set the statue in its place, did so with a purpose. It is for us to see that there lies no taint behind our pleasures; but even if this be not the message, the heart of the mystery, may not the figure stand perhaps for the end, the bitter end, which lies ahead of all, when the lip is silent and the eye shut, and the heart is stilled at last?

The quiet figure with its secret, wicked smile, somehow slurred for me the sunshine and the pleasant flowers, and I was glad when we turned away.— Ever yours,

T. B.

UPTON,
June 11, 1904.

DEAR HERBERT,—Yes, I am sure you are right. The thing I get more and more impatient of every year is conventionality in every form. It is rather foolish, I am well aware, to be impatient about anything; and great conventionality of mind is not inconsistent with entire sincerity, for the simple reason that conventionality is what ninety-nine hundredths of the human race enjoy. Most people have no wish to make up their own minds about anything; they do not care to know what they like or why they like it. This is often the outcome of a deep-seated modesty. The ordinary person says to himself, "Who am I that I should set up a standard? If all the people that I know like certain occupations and certain amusements, they are probably right, and I will try to like them too." I don't mean that this feeling is often put into words, but it is there; and there is for most people an immense power in habit. People grow to like what they do, and seldom inquire if they really like it, or why they like it.

Of course, to a certain extent, conventionality is a useful, peaceful thing. I am not here recommending eccentricity of any kind. People ought to fall in simply and quietly with ordinary modes of life, dress, and behaviour; it saves time and trouble; it sets the mind free. But what I rather mean is that, when the ordinary usages of life have been complied with, all sensible people ought to have a line of their own about occupation, amusements, friends, and not run to and fro like sheep just where the social current sets. What I mean is best explained by a couple of instances. I met at dinner last night our old acquaintance, Foster, who was at school with us. He was in my house; I don't think you ever knew much of him. He was a pleasant, good-humoured boy enough; but his whole mind was set on discovering the exact code of social school life. He wanted to play the right games, to wear the right clothes, to know the right people. He liked being what he called "in the swim." He never made friends with an obscure or unfashionable boy. He was quite pleasant to his associates when he was himself obscure; but he waited quietly for his opportunity to recommend himself to prominent boys, and, when the time came, he gently threw over all his old companions and struck out into more distinguished regions. He was never disagreeable or conceited; he merely dropped his humble friends until they too were approved as worthy of greater distinction, and then he took them up again. He succeeded in his ambitions, as most cool and clear-headed persons do. He became what would be called very popular; he gave himself no airs; he was always good company; he was never satirical or critical. The same thing has gone on ever since. He married a nice wife; he secured a good official position. Last night, as I say, I met him here. He came into the room with the same old pleasant smile, beautifully dressed, soberly appointed. His look and gestures were perfectly natural and appropriate. He has never made any attempt to see me or keep up old acquaintance; but here, where I have a certain standing and position, it was obviously the right thing to treat me with courteous deference. He came up to me with a genial welcome, and, but for a little touch of prosperous baldness, I could have imagined that he was hardly a day older than when he was a boy. He reminded me of some cheerful passages of boyhood; he asked with kindly interest after my work; he paid me exactly the right compliments; and I became aware that I was, for the moment, one of the pawns in his game, to be delicately pushed about where it suited him. We talked of other matters; he held exactly the right political opinions, a mild and cautious liberalism; he touched on the successes of certain politicians and praised them appropriately; he deplored the failure of certain old friends in political life. "A very good fellow," he said of Hughes, "but just a little—what shall I say?—impracticable?" He had seen all the right plays, heard the right music, read the right books. He deplored the obscurity of George Meredith, but added that he was an undoubted genius. He confessed himself to be an ardent admirer of Wagner; he thought Elgar a man of great power; but he had not made up his mind about Strauss. I found that "not making up his mind about" a person was one of his favourite expressions. If he sees that some man is showing signs of vigour and originality in any department of life, he keeps his eye upon him; if he passes safely through the shallows, he praises him, saying that he has watched his rise; if he fails, our friend will be ready with the reasons for his failure, adding that he always feared that so-and-so was a little unpractical.

I can't describe to you the dreariness and oppression that fell upon me. The total absence of generosity, of independent interest, weighed on my soul. The one quality that this equable and judicious critic was on the look-out for was the power of being approved. Foster's view seemed to knock the bottom out of life, to deprive everything equally of charm and individuality.

The conversation turned on golf, and one of the guests, whom I am shortly about to describe, said bluffly that he considered golf and drink to be the two curses of the country. Our polite friend turned courteously towards him, treated the remark as an excellent sally, and then said that he feared he must himself plead guilty to a great devotion to golf. "You see all kinds of pleasant people," he said, "in such a pleasant way; and then it tempts one into the open air; and it is such an excellent investment, in the way of exercise, for one's age; a man can play a very decent game till he is sixty—though, of course, it is no doubt a little overdone." We all felt that he was right; he took the rational, the sensible view; but it tempted me, though I successfully resisted the temptation, to express an exaggerated dislike of golf which I do not feel.

The guest whose remark had occasioned this discourse is one of my colleagues, Murchison by name—you don't know him—a big, rugged, shy, sociable fellow, who is in many ways one of the best masters here. He is always friendly, amusing, courteous. He holds strong opinions, which he does not produce unless the occasion demands it. He keeps a good deal to himself, follows his own pursuits, and knows his own mind. He is very tolerant, and can get on with almost everybody. The boys respect him, like his teaching, think him clever, sensible, and amusing. There are a great many things about which he knows nothing, and is always ready to confess his ignorance. But whenever he does understand a subject, and he has a strong taste for art and letters, you always feel that his thoughts and opinions are fresh and living. They are not produced like sardines from a tin, with a painful similarity and regularity. He has strong prejudices, for which he can always give a reason; but he is always ready to admit that it is a matter of taste. He does not tilt in a Quixotic manner at established things, but he goes along trying to do his work in the best manner attainable. He is no genius, and his character is by no means a perfect one; he has pronounced faults, of which he is perfectly conscious, and which he never attempts to disguise. But he is simple, straightforward, affectionate, and sincere. If he were more courageous, more fiery, he would be, I think, a really great man; but this he somehow misses.

The two men, Foster and Murchison, are as great a contrast as can well be imagined. They serve to illustrate exactly what I mean. Our friend Foster is perfectly correct and admirably pleasant. You would never think of confiding in him, or saying to him what you really felt; but, on the other hand, there is no one whom I would more willingly consult in a small and delicate point of practical conduct—and his advice would be excellent.

But Murchison is a real man; he knows his limitations, but he takes nothing second-hand. He brings his own mind and character to bear on every problem, and judges people and things on their own merits.

Of course one does not desire that conventional people should strive after unconventionality. That produces the most sickening conventionality of all, because it is merely an attempt to construct a pose that shall be accepted as unconventional. The only thing is to be natural; and, after all, if one merely desires to see how the cat jumps and then to jump after it, it is better to do so frankly and make no pretence about it.

But I am sure that it is one's duty as a teacher to try and show boys that no opinions, no tastes, no emotions are worth much unless they are one's own. I suffered acutely as a boy from the lack of being shown this. I found—I am now speaking of intellectual things—that certain authors were held up to me as models which I was unfortunate enough to dislike. Instead of making up my own mind about it, instead of trying to see what I did admire and why I admired it, I tried feebly for years to admire what I was told was admirable. The result was waste of time and confusion of thought. In the same way I followed feebly, as a boy, after the social code. I tried to like the regulation arrangements, and thought dimly that I was in some way to blame because I did not. Not until I went up to Cambridge did the conception of mental liberty steal upon me—and then only partly. Of course if I had had more originality I should have perceived this earlier. But the world appeared to me a great, organised, kindly conspiracy, which must be joined, in however feeble a spirit. I have learnt gradually that, after a decent compliance with superficial conventionalities, there are not only no penalties attached to independence, but that there, and there alone, is happiness to be found; and that the rewards of a free judgement and an authentic admiration are among the best and highest things that the world has to bestow....—Ever yours,

T. B.

UPTON,
June 18, 1904.

DEAR HERBERT,—I am sick at heart. I received one of those letters this morning which are the despair of most schoolmasters. I have in my house a boy aged seventeen, who is absolutely alone in the world. He has neither father or mother, brother or sister. He spends his holidays with an aunt, a clever and charming person, but a sad invalid (by the way, in passing, what a wretched thing in English it is that there is no female of the word "man"; "woman" means something quite different, and always sounds slightly disrespectful; "lady" is impossible, except in certain antique phrases). The boy is frail, intellectual, ungenial. He is quite incapable of playing games decently, having neither strength or aptitude; he finds it hard to make friends, and the consequence is that, like all clever people who don't meet with any success, he takes refuge in a kind of contemptuous cynicism. His aunt is devoted to him and to his best interests, but she is too much of an invalid to be able to look after him; the result is that he is allowed practically to do exactly as he likes in the holidays; he hates school cordially, and I don't wonder. He fortunately has one taste, and that is for science, and it is more than a taste, it is a real passion. He does not merely dabble about with chemicals, or play tricks with electricity; but he reads dry, hard, abstruse science, and writes elaborate monographs, which I read with more admiration than comprehension. This is almost his only hold on ordinary life, and I encourage it with all my might; I ask about his work, make such suggestions as I can, and praise his successful experiments and his treatises, so far as I can understand them, loudly and liberally.

This morning one of his guardians writes to me about him. He is a country gentleman, with a large estate, who married a cousin of my pupil. He is a big, pompous, bumble-bee kind of man, who prides himself on speaking his mind, and is quite unaware that it is only his position that saves him from the plainest retorts. He writes to say that he is much exercised about his ward's progress. The boy, he says, is fanciful and delicate, and has much too good an opinion of himself. That is true; and he goes on to lay down the law as to what he "needs." He must be thrown into the society of active and vigorous boys; he must play games; he must go to the gymnasium. And then he must learn self-reliance; he must not be waited upon; he must be taught that it is his business to be considerate of others; he must learn to be obliging, and to look after other people. He goes on to say that all he wants is the influence of a strong and sensible man (that is a cut at me), and he will be obliged if I will kindly attend to the matter.

Well, what does he want me to do? Does he expect me to run races with the boy? To introduce him to the captain of the eleven? To have him thrust into teams of cricket and football from which his incapacity for all games naturally excludes him? When our bumble-bee friend was at school himself—and a horrid boy he must have been—what would he have said if a master had told him to put a big, clumsy, and incapable boy into a house cricket eleven in order to bring him out?

Then as to teaching him to be considerate, the mischief is all done in the holidays; the boy is not waited on here, and he has plenty of vigorous discipline in the kind of barrack life the boys lead. Does he expect me to march into the boy's home, and request that the boy may black his own boots and carry up the coals!

The truth is that the man has no real policy; he sees the boy's deficiencies, and liberates his mind by requesting me, as if I were a kind of tradesman, to see that they are corrected.

Of course the temptation is to write the man an acrimonious letter, and to point out the idiotic character of his suggestions. But that is worse than useless.

What I have done is to write and say that I have received his kind and sensible letter, that he has laid his finger on the exact difficulties, and that naturally I am anxious to put them straight. I then added that his own recollection of his school-days will show that one cannot help a boy in athletic or social matters beyond a certain point, that one can only see that a boy has a fair chance, and is not overlooked, but that other boys would not tolerate (and I know that he does not mean to suggest this) that a boy should be included in a team for which he is unfit, simply in order that his social life should be encouraged. I then point out that as to discipline there is no lack of it here; and that it is only at home that he is spoilt; and that I hope he will use his influence, in a region where I cannot do more than make suggestions, to minimise the evil.

The man will approve of the letter; he will think me sensible and himself extraordinarily wise.

Does that seem to you to be cynical? I don't think it is. The man is sincerely anxious for the boy's welfare, just as I am, and we had better agree than disagree. The fault of his letter is that it is stupid, and that it is offensive. The former quality I can forgive, and the latter is only stupidity in another form. He thinks in his own mind that if I am paid to educate the boy I ought to be glad of advice, that I ought to be grateful to have things that I am not likely to detect for myself pointed out by an enlightened and benevolent man.

Meanwhile I shall proceed to treat the boy on my own theory. I don't expect him to play games; I don't think that it is, humanly speaking, possible to expect a sensitive, frail boy to continue to play a game in which he only makes himself ridiculous and contemptible from first to last. Of course if a boy who is incapable of success in athletics does go on playing games perseveringly and good-humouredly, he gets a splendid training, and, as a rule, conciliates respect. But this boy could not do that.

Then I shall try to encourage the boy in any taste he may exhibit, and try to build up a real structure on these slender lines. The great point is that he shall have SOME absorbing and wholesome instinct. He will be wealthy, and in a position to gratify any whim. He is not in the least likely to do anything foolish or vicious—he has not got the animal spirits for that. I shall encourage him to take up politics; and I shall try to put into his head a desire to do something for his fellow-creatures, and not to live an entirely lonely and self-absorbed life.

I have a theory that in education it is better to encourage aptitudes than to try merely to correct deficiencies. One can't possibly extirpate weaknesses by trying to crush them. One must build up vitality and interest and capacity. It is like the parable of the evil spirits. It is of no use simply to cast them out and leave the soul empty and swept; one must encourage some strong, good spirit to take possession; one must build on the foundations that are there.

The boy is delicate-minded, able and intelligent; he is an interesting companion, when he is once at his ease. If only this busy, fussy, hearty old bore would leave him alone! What I am afraid of his doing is of his getting the boy to stay with him, making him go out hunting, and laughing mercilessly at his tumbles. The misery that a stupid, genial man can inflict upon a sensitive boy like this is dreadful to contemplate.

At the end of the half I shall write a letter about the boy's work, and delicately hint that, if he is encouraged in his subject, he may attain high distinction and eventually rise to political or scientific eminence. The old bawler will take the fly with a swirl—see if he does not! And, if I can secure an interview with him, I will wager that my triumph will be complete.

Does this all seem very dingy to you, my dear Herbert? You have never had to deal with tiresome, stupid people in a professional capacity, you see. There is a distinct pleasure in getting one's own way, in triumphing over an awkward situation, in leading an old buffer by the nose to do the thing which you think right, and to make him believe that you are all the time following his advice and treasuring up his precepts. But I can honestly say that my chief desire is not to amuse myself with this kind of diplomacy, but the real welfare of the child. I know you will believe that.—Ever yours,

T. B.

UPTON,
June 25, 1904.

DEAR HERBERT,—This is not a letter; it is a sketch, an aquarelle out of my portfolio.

Yesterday was a hot, heavy, restless day, with thunder brewing in the dark heart of huge inky clouds; a day when one craves for light, and brisk airs, and cold bare hill-tops; when one desires to get away from one's kind, away from close rooms and irritable persons. So I went off on my patient and uncomplaining bicycle, along a country road; and then crossing a wide common, like the field, I thought, in the Pilgrim's Progress across which Evangelist pointed an improving finger, I turned down to the left to the waterside In the still air, that seemed to listen, the blue wooded hills across the river had a dim, rich beauty. How mysterious are the fields and heights from which one is separated by a stream, the fields in which one knows every tree and sloping lawn by sight, and where one sets foot so rarely! The road came to an end in a little grassy space among high-branching elms. On my left was a farm, with barns and byres, overhung by stately walnut trees; on the right a grange among its great trees, a low tiled house, with white casements, in a pleasant garden, full of trellised roses, a big dovecote, with a clattering flight of wheeling pigeons circling round and round. Hard by, close to the river, stands a little ancient church, with a timbered spire, the trees growing thickly about it, dreaming forgotten dreams.

Here all was still and silent; the very children moved languidly about, not knowing what ailed them. Far off across the wide-watered plain came a low muttering of thunder, and a few big drops pattered in the great elms.

This secluded river hamlet has an old history; the church, which is served from a distant parish, stands in a narrow strip of land which runs down across the fields to the river, and dates from the time when the river was a real trade-highway, and when neighbouring parishes, which had no frontages on the stream, found it convenient to have a wharf to send their produce, timber or bricks, away by water. But the wharf has long since perished, though a few black stakes show where it stood; and the village, having no landing-place and no inn, has dropped out of the river life, and minds its own quiet business.

A few paces from the church the river runs silently and strongly to the great weir below. To-day it was swollen with rain and turbid, and plucked steadily at the withies. To-day the stream, which is generally full of life, was almost deserted. But it came into my head what an allegory it made. Here through the unvisited meadows, with their huge elms, runs this thin line of glittering vivid life; you hear, hidden in dark leaves, the plash of oars, the grunt of rowlocks, and the chatter of holiday folk, to whom the river-banks are but a picture through which they pass, and who know nothing of the quiet fields that surround them. That, I thought, following a train of reflection, is like life itself, moving in its bright, familiar channel, so unaware of the broad tracts of mystery that hem it in. May there not be presences, unseen, who look down wondering—as I look to-day through my screen of leafy boughs—on the busy-peopled stream that runs so merrily between its scarped banks of clay? I know not; yet it seems as though it might be so.

Beneath the weir, with its fragrant, weedy scent, where the green river plunges and whitens through the sluices, lies a deep pool, haunted by generations of schoolboys, who wander, flannelled and straw-hatted, up through the warm meadows to bathe. In such sweet memories I have my part, when one went riverwards with some chosen friend, speaking with the cheerful frankness of boyhood of all our small concerns, and all we meant to do; and then the cool grass under the naked feet, the delicious recoil of the fresh, tingling stream, and the quiet stroll back into the ordered life so full of simple happiness.

"Ah! happy fields, ah! pleasing shade,
    Ah! fields beloved in vain!"

sang the sad poet of Eton—but not in vain, I think, for these old beautiful memories are not sad; the good days are over and gone, and they cannot be renewed; but they are like a sweet spring of youth, whose waters fail not, in which a tired soul may bathe and be clean again. They may bring back

"The times when I remember to have been
   Joyful, and free from blame."

To be pensive, not sentimental, is the joy of later life. The thought of the sweet things that have had an end, of life lived out and irrevocable, is not a despairing thought, unless it is indulged with an unavailing regret. It is rather to me a sign that, whatever we may be or become, we are surrounded with the same quiet beauty and peace, if we will but stretch out our hands and open our hearts to it. To grow old patiently and bravely, even joyfully—that is the secret; and it is as idle to repine for the lost joys as it would have been in the former days to repine because we were not bigger and stronger and more ambitious. Life, if it does not become sweeter, becomes more interesting; fresh ties are formed, fresh paths open out; and there should come, too, a simple serenity of living, a certainty that, whatever befall, we are in wise and tender hands.

So I reasoned with myself beside the little holy church, not far from the moving stream.

But the time warned me to be going. The thunder had drawn off to the west; a faint breeze stirred and whispered in the elms. The day declined. But I had had my moment, and my heart was full; for it is such moments as these that are the pure gold of life, when the scene and the mood move together to some sweet goal in perfect unison. Sometimes the scene is there without the mood, or the mood comes and finds no fitting pasturage; but to-day, both were mine; and the thought, echoing like a strain of rich sad music, passed beyond the elms, beyond the blue hills, back to its mysterious home....

There, that is the end of my sketch; a little worked up, but substantially true. Tell me if you like the kind of thing; if you do, it is rather a pleasure to write thus occasionally. But it may seem to you to be affected, and, in that case, I won't send you any more of such reveries.

You seem very happy and prosperous; but then you like heat, and enjoy it like a lizard. My love to all of you.—Ever yours,

T. B.

UPTON,
July 1, 1904.

DEAR HERBERT,—What you say about forming habits is very interesting. It is quite true that one gets very little done without a certain method; and it is equally true that, if one does manage to arrive at a certain definite programme for one's life and work, it is very easy to get a big task done. Just reflect on this fact; it would not be difficult, in any life, to so arrange things that one could write a short passage every day, say enough to fill a page of an ordinary octavo. Well, if one stuck to it, that would mean that in the course of a year one would have a volume finished. Sometimes my colleagues express surprise that I can find time for so much literary work; and on the other hand if I tell them how much time I am able to devote to it they are equally surprised that I can get anything done, because it seems so little. This is the fact; I can get an hour—possibly two—on Tuesday, two hours on Thursday, one on Friday, two on Saturday, and one or two on Sunday—nine hours a week under favourable circumstances, and never a moment more. But writing being to me the purest pleasure and refreshment, I never lose a minute in getting to work, and I use every moment of the time. That does not include reading; but by dint of having books about, and by working carefully, so that I do not need to go over the same ground twice, I get through a good deal in the week. I have trained myself, too, to be able to write at full speed when I am at work, and I can count on writing three octavo pages in an hour, or even four. The result is, as you will see, that in a term of twelve weeks, I can turn out between three and four hundred pages. The curious thing is that I do better original work in the term-time than in the holidays. I think the pressure of a good deal of mechanical work, not of an exhausting kind, clears the brain and makes it vigorous. Of course it is rather scrappy work; but I lay my plans in the holidays, make my skeleton, and work up my authorities; and so I can go ahead at full steam.

But I have strayed away from the subject of habits; and the moral of the above is only that habits are easy enough if you like the task enough. If I did not care for writing, I should find abundance of excellent reasons why I should not do it.

Pater says somewhere that forming habits is failure in life; by which I suppose he means that if one gets tied down to a petty routine of one's own, it generally ends in one's becoming petty too—narrow-minded and conventional. I don't suppose he referred to method, because he was one of the most methodical of men. He wrote down sentences that came into his mind, scattered ideas, on small cards; when he had a sufficient store of these, he sorted them and built up his essay out of them.

But I am equally aware that habit is apt to become very tyrannical indeed, if it is acquired. In my own case I have got into the habit of writing only between tea and dinner, owing to its being the only time at my disposal, so that I can hardly write at any other time; and that is inconvenient in the holidays. Moreover, I like writing so much, enjoy the shaping of sentences so intensely, that I tend to arrange my day in the holidays entirely with a view to having these particular hours free for writing; and thus for a great part of the year I lose the best and most enjoyable part of the day, the sweet summer evenings, when the tired world grows fragrant and cool.

One ought to have a routine for home life certainly; but it is not wholesome when one begins to grudge the slightest variation from the programme. I speak philosophically, because I am in the grip of the evil myself. The reason why I care so little for staying anywhere, and even for travelling, is because it disarranges my plan of the day, and I don't feel certain of being able to secure the time for writing which I love. But this is wrong; it is vivendi perdere causas, and I think we ought resolutely to court a difference of life at intervals, and to learn to bear with equanimity the suspension of one's daily habits. You are certainly wise, if you find it suits you, to secure the morning for writing. Personally my mind is not at its best then; it is dulled and weakened by sleep, and it requires the tonic of routine work and bodily exercise before it expands and flourishes.

Another grievous tendency which grows on me is an incapacity for idleness. That will amuse you, when you remember the long evenings at Eton which we used to spend in vacant talk. I remember so well your saying after tea one evening, in that poky room of yours with the barred windows at the end of the upper passage, "How delightful to think that there are four hours with nothing whatever to do!" Do you remember, too, that night when we sate at tea, blissfully, wholesomely tired after a college match? John and Ellen, those strange, gruff beings, came in to wash up, carrying that horrible, steaming can of tea-dregs in which our cups were plunged: they cleared the table as we sate; it was over before six, and it was not till the prayer-bell rang at 9.30 that we became aware we had sate the whole evening with the table between us. What DID we talk about? I wish to Heaven I could sit and talk like that now! That is another thing which grows upon me, my dislike of mere chatting: it is not priggish to say it, because I regret and abominate my stupidity in that respect. But there is nothing now which induces more rapid and more desperate physical fatigue than to sit still and know I have to pump up talk for an hour.

The moral of all this is that YOU must take good care to form habits, and *I* must take care to unform them. YOU must resist the temptation to read the papers, to stroll, to talk to your children; and *I* must try to cultivate leisurely propensities. I think that, as a schoolmaster, one might do very good work as a peripatetic talker. I have a big garden here—to think that you have never seen it!—with a great screen of lilacs and some pleasant gravel walks. I never enter it, I am afraid. But if in the pleasant summer I could learn the art of sitting there, of having tea there, and making a few boys welcome if they cared to come, it would be good for all of us, and would give the boys some pleasant memories. I don't think there is anything gives me a pleasanter thrill than to recollect the times I spent as a boy in old Hayward's garden. He told me and Francis Howard that we might go and sit there if we liked. You were not invited, and I never dared to ask him. It was a pleasant little place, with a lawn surrounded with trees, and a summer-house full of armchairs, with an orchard behind it—now built over. Howard and I used at one time to go there a good deal, to read and talk. I remember him reading Shakespeare's sonnets aloud, though I had not an idea what they were all about—but his rich, resonant voice comes back to me now; and then he showed me a MS. book of his own poems. Ye Gods, how great I thought them! I copied many of them out and have them still. Hayward used to come strolling about; I can see him standing there in a big straw hat, with his hands behind him, like the jolly old leisurely fellow he was. "Don't get up, boys," he used to say. Once or twice he sate with us, and talked lazily about some book we were reading. He never took any trouble to entertain us, but I used to feel that we were welcome, and that it really pleased him that we cared to come. Now he lives in a suburb, on a pension: why do I never go to see him?

"La, Perry, how yer do run on!" as the homely Warden's wife said to the voluble Chaplain. I never meant to write you such a letter; but I am glad indeed to find you really settling down. We must cultivate our garden, as Voltaire said; and I only wish that the garden of my own spirit were more full of "shelter and fountains," and less stocked with long rows of humble vegetables; but there are a few flowers here and there.—Ever yours,

T. B.

MONK'S ORCHARD, UPTON,
July 11, 1904.

MY DEAR HERBERT,—I am going to pour out a pent-up woe. I have just escaped from a very fatiguing experience. I said good-bye this morning, with real cordiality, to a thoroughly uncongenial and disagreeable visitor. You will probably be surprised when I tell you his name, because he is a popular, successful, and, many people hold, a very agreeable man. It is that ornament of the Bar, Mr. William Welbore, K.C. His boy is in my house; and Mr. Welbore (who is a widower) invited himself to stay a Sunday with me in the tone of one who, if anything, confers a favour. I had no real reason for refusing, and, to speak truth, any evasion on my part would have been checked by the boy.

It is a fearful bore here to have any one staying in the house at all, unless he is so familiar an old friend that you can dispense with all ceremony. I have no guest-rooms to speak of; and a guest is always in my study when I want to be there, talking when I want to work, or wanting to smoke at inconvenient times. One's study is also one's office; boys keep dropping in, and, when I have an unperceptive guest, I have to hold interviews with boys wherever I can—in passages and behind doors. What made it worse was that it was a wet Sunday, so that my visitor sate with me all day, and I have no doubt thought he was enlivening a dull professional man with some full-flavoured conversation. Then one has to arrange for separate meals; when I am alone I never, as you know, have dinner, but go in to the boys' supper and have a slice of cold meat. But on this occasion I had to have a dinner-party on Saturday and another on Sunday; and the breakfast hour, when I expect to read letters and the paper, was taken up with general conversation. I am ashamed to think how much discomposed I was; but a schoolmaster is practically always on duty. I wonder how Mr.

Welbore would have enjoyed the task of entertaining me for a day or two in his chambers! But one ought not, I confess, to be so wedded to one's own habits; and I feel, when I complain, rather like the rich gentleman who said to John Wesley, when his fire smoked, "These are some of the crosses, Mr. Wesley, that I have to bear."

I could have stood it with more equanimity if only Mr. Welbore had been a congenial guest. But even in the brief time at my disposal I grew to dislike him with an intensity of which I am ashamed. I hated his clothes, his boots, his eye-glass, the way he cleared his throat, the way he laughed. He is a successful, downright, blunt, worldly man, and is generally called a good fellow by his friends. He arrived in time for tea on Saturday; he talked about his boy a little; the man is in this case, unlike Wordsworth's hero, the father of the child; and the boy will grow up exactly like him. Young Welbore does his work punctually and without interest; he plays games respectably; he likes to know the right boys; he is not exactly disagreeable, but he derides all boys who are in the least degree shy, stupid, or unconventional. He is quite a little man of the world, in fact. Well, I don't like that type of creature, and I tried to indicate to the father that I thought the boy was rather on the wrong lines. He heard me with impatience, as though I was bothering him about matters which belonged to my province; and he ended by laughing, not very agreeably, and saying: "Well, you don't seem to have much of a case against Charlie; he appears to be fairly popular. I confess that I don't much go in for sentiment in education; if a boy does his work, and plays his games, and doesn't get into trouble, I think he is on the right lines." And then he paid me an offensive compliment: "I hear you make the boys very comfortable, and I am sure I am obliged to you for taking so much interest in him." He then went off for a little to see the boy. He appeared at dinner, and I had invited two or three of the most intelligent of my colleagues. Mr. Welbore simply showed off. He told stories; he made mirthless legal jokes. One of my colleagues, Patrick, a man of some originality, ventured to dispute an opinion of Mr. Welbore's, and Mr. Welbore turned him inside out, by a series of questions, as if he was examining a witness, in a good-natured, insolent way, and ended by saying: "Well, Mr. Patrick, that sort of thing wouldn't do in a law-court, you know; you would have to know your subject better than that." I was not surprised, after dinner, at the alacrity with which my colleagues quitted the scene, on all sorts of professional excuses. Then Mr. Welbore sate up till midnight, smoking strong cigars, and giving me his ideas on the subject of education. That was a bitter pill, for he worsted me in every argument I undertook.

Sunday was a nightmare day; every spare moment was given up to Mr. Welbore. I breakfasted with him, took him to chapel, took him to the boys' luncheon, walked with him, sate with him, talked with him. The strain was awful. The man sees everything from a different point of view to my own. One ought to be able to put up with that, of course, and I don't at all pretend that I consider my point of view better than his; but I had to endure the consciousness that he thought his own point of view in all respects superior to mine. He thought me a slow-coach, an old maid, a sentimentalist; and I had, too, the galling feeling that on the whole he approved of a drudge like myself taking a rather priggish point of view, and that he did not expect a schoolmaster to be a man of the world, any more than he would have expected a curate or a gardener to be. I felt that the man was in his way a worse prig even than I was, and even more of a Pharisee, because he judged everything by a certain conventional standard. His idea of life was a place where you found out what was the right thing to do; and that if you did that, money and consideration, the only two things worth having, followed as a matter of course. "Of course he's not my sort," was the way in which he dismissed almost the only person we discussed whom I thoroughly admired. So we went on; and I can only say that the relief I felt when I saw him drive away on Monday morning was so great as almost to make it worth while having endured his visit. I think he rather enjoyed himself—at least he threatened to pay me another visit; and I am sure he had the benevolent consciousness of having brought a breath of the big world into a paltry life. The big world! what a terrible place it would be if it was peopled by Welbores! My only consolation is that men of his type don't achieve the great successes. They are very successful up to a certain point; they get what they want. Welbore will be a judge before long, and he has already made a large fortune. But there is a demand for more wisdom and generosity in the great places—at least I hope so. Welbore's idea of the world is a pleasant place where such men as he can make money and have a good time. He thinks art, religion, beauty, poetry, music, all stuff. I would not mind that if only he did not KNOW it was stuff. God forbid that we should pretend to enjoy such things if we do not—and, after all, the man is not a hypocrite. But his view is that any one who is cut in a different mould is necessarily inferior; and what put the crowning touch to my disgust was that on Sunday afternoon we met a Cabinet Minister, who is a great student of literature. He talked about books to Mr. Welbore, and Mr. Welbore heard him with respect, because the Minister was in the swim. He said afterwards to me that people's foibles were very odd; but he so far respected the Minister's success as to think that he had a right to a foible. He would have crushed one of my colleagues who had battled in the same way, with a laugh and a few ugly words.

Well, let me dismiss Mr. Welbore from my mind. The worst of it is that, though I don't agree with him, he has cast a sort of blight on my mind. It is as though I had seen him spit on the face of a statue that I loved. I don't like vice in any shape; but I equally dislike a person who has a preference for manly vices over sentimental ones; and the root of Mr. Welbore's dislike of vice is simply that it tends to interfere with the hard sort of training which is necessary for success.

Mr. Welbore, as a matter of fact, seems to me really to augur worse for the introduction of the kingdom of heaven upon earth than any number of drunkards and publicans. One feels that the world is so terribly strong, stronger even than sin; and what is worse, there seems to be so little in the scheme of things that could ever give Mr. Welbore the lie.—Ever yours,

T. B

UPTON,
July 16, 1904.

DEAR HERBERT,—I declare that the greatest sin there is in the world is stupidity. The character that does more harm in the world than any other is the character in which stupidity and virtue are combined. I grow every day more despondent about the education we give at our so-called classical schools. Here, you know, we are severely classical; and to have to administer such a system is often more than I can bear with dignity or philosophy. One sees arrive here every year a lot of brisk, healthy boys, with fair intelligence, and quite disposed to work; and at the other end one sees depart a corresponding set of young gentlemen who know nothing, and can do nothing, and are profoundly cynical about all intellectual things. And this is the result of the meal of chaff we serve out to them week after week; we collect it, we chop it up, we tie it up in packets; we spend hours administering it in teaspoons, and this is the end. I am myself the victim of this kind of education; I began Latin at seven and Greek at nine, and, when I left Cambridge, I did not know either of them well. I could not sit in an arm-chair and read either a Greek or a Latin book, and I had no desire to do it. I knew a very little French, a very little mathematics, a very little science; I knew no history, no German, no Italian. I knew nothing of art or music; my ideas of geography were childish. And yet I am decidedly literary in my tastes, and had read a lot of English for myself. It is nothing short of infamous that any one should, after an elaborate education, have been so grossly uneducated. My only accomplishment was the writing of rather pretty Latin verse.

And yet this preposterous system continues year after year. I had an animated argument with some of the best of my colleagues the other day about it. I cannot tell you how profoundly irritating these wiseacres were. They said all the stock things—that one must lay a foundation, and that it could only be laid by using the best literatures; that Latin was essential because it lay at the root of so many other languages; and Greek, because there the human intellect had reached its high-water mark,—"and it has such a noble grammar," one enthusiastic Grecian said; that an active-minded person could do all the rest for himself. It was in vain to urge that in many cases the whole foundation was insecure; and that all desire to raise a superstructure was eliminated. My own belief is that Greek and Latin are things to be led up to, not begun with; that they are hard, high literatures, which require an initiation to comprehend; and that one ought to go backwards in education, beginning with what one knows.

It seems to me, to use a similitude, that the case is thus. If one lives in a plain and wishes to reach a point upon a hill, one must make a road from the plain upwards. It will be a road at the base, it will be a track higher up, and a path at last, used only by those who have business there. But the classical theorists seem to me to make an elaborate section of macadamised road high in the hills, and, having made it, to say that the people who like can make their own road in between.

How would I mend all this? Well, I would change methods in the first place. If one wanted to teach a boy French or German effectively, so that he would read and appreciate, one would dispense with much of the grammar, except what was absolutely necessary. In the case of classics it is all done the other way; grammar is a subject in itself; boys have to commit to memory long lists of words and forms which they never encounter; they have to acquire elaborate analyses of different kinds of usages, which are of no assistance in dealing with the language itself. It is beginning with the wrong end of the stick. Grammar is the scientific or philosophical theory of language; it may be an interesting and valuable study for a mind of strong calibre, but it does not help one to understand an author or to appreciate a style.

Then, too, I would sweep away for all but boys of special classical ability most kinds of composition. Fancy teaching a boy side by side with the elements of German or French to compose German and French verse, heroic, Alexandrine, or lyrical! The idea has only to be stated to show its fatuity. I would teach boys to write Latin prose, because it is a tough subject, and it initiates them into the process of disentangling the real sense of the English copy. But I would abolish all Latin verse composition, and all Greek composition of every kind for mediocre boys. Not only would they learn the languages much faster, but there would be a great deal of time saved as well. Then I would abolish the absurd little lessons, with the parsing, and I would at all hazards push on till they could read fluently.

Of course the above improvement of methods is sketched on the hypothesis that both Greek and Latin are retained. Personally I would retain Latin for most, but give up Greek altogether in the majority of cases. I would teach all boys French thoroughly. I would try to make them read and write it easily, and that should be the linguistic staple of their education. Then I would teach them history, mainly modern English history, and modern geography; a very little mathematics and elementary science. Such boys would be, in my belief, well-educated; and they would never be tempted to disbelieve in the usefulness of their education.

When I propound these ideas, my colleagues talk of soft options, and of education without muscle or nerve. My retort is that the majority of boys educated on classical lines are models of intellectual debility as it is. They are uninterested, cynical, and they cannot even read or write the languages which they have been so carefully taught.

What I want is experiment of every kind; but my cautious friends say that one would only get something a great deal worse. That I deny. I maintain that it is impossible to have anything worse, and that the majority of the boys we turn out are intellectually in so negative a condition that any change would be an improvement.

But I effect nothing; nothing is attempted, nothing done. I do my best— fortunately our system admits of that—to teach my private pupils a little history, and I make them write essays. The results are decidedly encouraging; but meanwhile my colleagues go on in the old ways, quite contented, pathetically conscientious, laboriously slaving away, and apparently not disquieted by results.

I am very near the end of my tether—one cannot go on for ever administering a system in which one has lost all faith. If there were signs of improvement I should be content. If our headmaster would even insist upon the young men whom he appoints obtaining a competent knowledge of French and German before they come here it would be something, because then, when the change is made, there would be less friction. But even a new headmaster with liberal ideas would now be hopelessly hampered by the fact that he would have a staff who could not teach modern subjects at all, who knew nothing but classics, and classics only for teaching purposes.

It does me good to pour out my woes to you; I feel my position most acutely at this time of year, when the serious business of the place is cricket. In cricket the boys are desperately and profoundly interested, not so much in the game, as in the social rewards of playing it well. And my worthy colleagues give themselves to athletics with an earnestness which depresses me into real dejection. One meets a few of these beloved men at dinner; a few half-hearted remarks are made about politics and books; a good deal of vigorous gossip is talked; but if a question as to the best time for net-practice, or the erection of a board for the purpose of teaching slip-catches is mentioned, a profound seriousness falls on the group. A man sits up in his chair and speaks with real conviction and heat, with grave gestures. "The afternoon," he says, "is NOT a good time for nets; the boys are not at their best, and the pros. are less vigorous after their dinner. Whatever arrangements are made as to the times for school, the evening MUST be given up to nets."

The result is a pedantry, a priggishness, a solemnity about games which is simply deplorable. The whole thing seems to me to be distorted and out of proportion. I am one of those feeble people to whom exercise is only a pleasure and a recreation. If I don't like a game I don't play it. I do not see why I should be bored by my recreations. An immense number of boys are bored by their games, but they dare not say so because public opinion is so strong. As the summer goes on they avail themselves of every excuse to give up the regular games; and almost the only boys who persevere are boys who are within reach of some coveted "colour," which gives them social importance. What I desire is that boys should be serious about their work in a practical, business-like way, and amused by their games. As a matter of fact they are serious about games and profoundly bored by their work. The work is a relief from the tension of games, and if it were wholly given up, and games were played from morning to night, many boys would break down under the strain. I don't expect all the boys to be enthusiastic about their work; all healthily constituted people prefer play to work, I myself not least. But I want them to believe in it and to be interested in it, in the way that a sensible professional man is interested in his work. What produces the cynicism about work so common in classical schools is that the work is of a kind which does not seem to lead anywhere, and classics are a painful necessity which the boys intend to banish from their mind as soon as they possibly can.

This is a melancholy jeremiad, I am well aware; but it is also a frame of mind which grows upon me; and, to come back to my original proposition, it is the stupidity of virtuous men which is responsible for the continuance of this arid, out-of-joint system.—Ever yours,

T. B.

UPTON,
July 22, 1904.

MY DEAR HERBERT,—... I took a lonely walk to-day, and returned through a new quarter of the town. When I first knew it, thirty years ago, there was a single house here—an old farm, with a pair of pretty gables of mellow brick, and a weathered, solid, brick garden-wall that ran along the road; an orchard below; all round were quiet fields; a fine row of elms stood at the end of the wall. It was a place of no great architectural merit, but it had grown old there, having been built with solidity and dignity, and having won a simple grace from the quiet influences of rain and wind and sun. Very gradually it became engulphed. First a row of villas came down to the farm, badly planned and coarsely coloured; then a long row of yellow-brick houses appeared on the other side, and the house began to wear a shy, regretful air, like a respectable and simple person who has fallen into vulgar company. To-day I find that the elms have been felled; the old wall, so strongly and firmly built, is half down; the little garden within is full of planks and heaps of brick, the box hedges trodden down, the flowers trampled underfoot; the house itself is marked for destruction.

It made me perhaps unreasonably sad. I know that population must increase, and that people had better live in convenient houses near their work. The town is prosperous enough; there is work in plenty and good wages. There is nothing over which a philanthropist and a social reformer ought not to rejoice. But I cannot help feeling the loss of a simple and beautiful thing, though I know it appealed to few people, and though the house was held to be inconvenient and out of date. I feel as if the old place must have acquired some sort of personality, and must be suffering the innocent pangs of disembodiment. I know that there is abundance of the same kind of simple beauty everywhere; and yet I feel that a thing which has taken so long to mature, and which has drunk in and appropriated so much sweetness from the gentle hands of nature, ought not so ruthlessly and yet so inevitably to suffer destruction.

But it brought home to me a deeper and a darker thing still—the sad change and vicissitude of things, the absence of any permanence in this life of ours. We enter it so gaily, and, as a child, one feels that it is eternal. That is in itself so strange—that the child himself, who is so late an inmate of the family home, so new a care to his parents, should feel that his place in the world is so unquestioned, and that the people and things that surround him are all part of the settled order of life. It was, indeed, to me as a child a strange shock to discover, as I did from old schoolroom books, that my mother herself had been a child so short a time before my own birth.

Then life begins to move on, and we become gradually, very gradually, conscious of the swift rush of things. People round us begin to die, and drop out of their places. We leave old homes that we have loved. We hurry on ourselves from school to college; we enter the world. Then, in such a life as my own has been, the lesson comes insistently near. Boys come under our care, little tender creatures; a few days seem to pass and they are young and dignified men; a few years later they return as parents, to see about placing boys of their own; and one can hardly trace the boyish lineaments in the firm-set, bearded faces of manhood.

Then our own friends begin to be called away; faster and faster runs the stream; anniversaries return with horrible celerity; and soon we know that we must die.

What is one to hold on to in such a swift flux of things? The pleasures we enjoy at first fade; we settle down by comfortable firesides; we pile the tables with beloved books; friends go and come; we acquire habits; we find out our real tastes. We learn the measure of our powers. And yet, however simple and clear our routine becomes, we are warned every now and then by sharp lessons that it is all on sufferance, that we have no continuing city; and we begin to see, some later, some earlier, that we must find something to hold on to, something eternal and everlasting in which we can rest. There must be some anchor of the soul. And then I think that many of us take refuge in a mere stoical patience; we drink our glass when it is filled, and if it stands empty we try not to complain.

Now I am turning out, so to speak, the very lining of my mind to you. The anchor cannot be a material one, for there is no security there; it cannot be purely intellectual, for that is a shifting thing too. The well of the spirit is emptied, gradually and tenderly; we must find out what the spring is that can fill it up. Some would say that one's faith could supply the need, and I agree in so far as I believe that it must be a species of faith, in a life where our whole being and ending is such an impenetrable mystery. But it must be a deeper faith even than the faith of a dogmatic creed; for that is shifting, too, every day, and the simplest creed holds some admixture of human temperament and human error.

To me there are but two things that seem to point to hope. The first is the strongest and deepest of human things, the power of love—not, I think, the more vehement and selfish forms of love, the desire of youth for beauty, the consuming love of the mother for the infant—for these have some physical admixture in them. But the tranquil and purer manifestations of the spirit, the love of a father for a son, of a friend for a friend; that love which can light up a face upon the edge of the dark river, and can smile in the very throes of pain. That seems to me the only thing which holds out a tender defiance against change and suffering and death.

And then there is the faith in the vast creative mind that bade us be; mysterious and strange as are its manifestations, harsh and indifferent as they sometimes seem, yet at worst they seem to betoken a loving purpose thwarted by some swift cross-current, like a mighty river contending with little obstacles. Why the obstacles should be there, and how they came into being, is dark indeed. But there is enough to make us believe in a Will that does its utmost, and that is assured of some bright and far-off victory.

A faith in God and a faith in Love; and here seems to me to lie the strength and power of the Christian Revelation. It is to these two things that Christ pointed men. Though overlaid with definition, with false motive, with sophistry, with pedantry, this is the deep secret of the Christian Creed; and if we dare to link our will with the Will of God, however feebly, however complainingly, if we desire and endeavour not to sin against love, not to nourish hate or strife, to hold out the hand again and again to any message of sympathy or trust, not to struggle for our own profit, not to reject tenderness, to believe in the good faith and the good-will of men, we are then in the way. We may make mistakes, we may fail a thousand times, but the key of heaven is in our hands....—Ever yours,

T. B.

UPTON,
July 29, 1904.

DEAR HERBERT,—You must forgive me if this is a very sentimental letter, but this is the day that, of all days in the year, is to me most full of pathos—the last day of the summer half. My heart is like a full sponge and must weep a little. The last few days have been full to the brim of work and bustle—reports to be written, papers to be looked over. Yesterday was a day of sad partings. Half-a-dozen boys are leaving; and I have tried my best to tell them the truth about themselves; to say something that would linger in their minds, and yet to do it in a tender and affectionate way. And some of these boys' hearts are full to bursting too. I remember as if it were yesterday the last meeting at Eton of a Debating Society of which I was a member. We were electing new members and passing votes of thanks. Scott, who was then President and, as you remember, Captain of the Eleven, sate in his high chair above the table; opposite him, with his minute-book, was Riddell, then Secretary—that huge fellow in the Eight, you recollect. The vote of thanks to the President was carried; he said a few words in a broken voice, and sate down; the Secretary's vote of thanks was proposed, and he, too, rose to make acknowledgment. In the middle of his speech we were attracted by a movement of the President. He put his head in his hands and sobbed aloud. Riddell stopped, faltered, looked round, and leaving his sentence unfinished, sate down, put his face on the book and cried like a child. I don't think there was a dry eye in the room. And these boys were not sentimental, but straightforward young men of the world, honest, and, if anything, rather contemptuous, I had thought, of anything emotional. I have never forgotten that scene, and have interpreted many things in the light of it.

Well, this morning I woke early and heard all the bustle of departure. Depression fell on me; soon I got up, with a blessed sense of leisure, breakfasted at my ease, saw one or two boys, special friends, who came to me very grave and wistful. Then I wrote letters and did business; and this afternoon—it is fearfully hot—I have been for a stroll through the deserted fields and street.

So another of these beautiful things which we call the summer half is over, never to be renewed. There has been some evil, of course. I wish I could think otherwise. But the tone is good, and there have been none of those revelations of darkness that poison the mind. There has been idleness (I don't much regret that), and of course the usual worries. But the fact remains that a great number of happy, sensible boys have been living perhaps the best hours of their life, with equal, pleasant friendships, plenty of games, some wholesome work and discipline to keep all sweet, with this exquisite background of old towers and high-branching elms, casting their shade over rich meadow-grass; the scene will come back to these boys in weary hours, perhaps in sun-baked foreign lands, perhaps in smoky offices—nay, even on aching deathbeds, parched with fever.

The whole place has an incredibly wistful air, as though it missed the young life that circulated all about it; as though it spread its beauties out to be used and enjoyed, and wondered why none came to claim them. As a counterpoise to this I like to think of all the happiness flowing into hundreds of homes; the father and mother waiting for the sound of the wheels that bring the boy back; the children who have gone down to the lodge to welcome the big brothers with shouts and kisses; and the boy himself, with all the dear familiar scene and home faces opening out before him. We ought not to grudge the loneliness here before the thought of all those old and blessed joys of life that are being renewed elsewhere.

But I am here, a lonely man, wondering and doubting and desiring I hardly know what. Some nearness of life, some children of my own. You are apt to think of yourself as shelved and isolated; yet, after all, you have the real thing—wife, children, and home. But, in my case, these boys who are dear to me have forgotten me already. Disguise it as I will, I am part of the sordid furniture of life that they have so gladly left behind, the crowded corridor, the bare-walled schoolroom, the ink-stained desk. They are glad to think that they have not to assemble to-morrow to listen to my prosing, to bear the blows of the uncle's tongue, as Horace says. They like me well enough—for a schoolmaster; I know some of them would even welcome me, with a timorous joy, to their own homes.

I have had the feeling of my disabilities brought home to me lately in a special way. There is a boy in my house that I have tried hard to make friends with. He is a big, overgrown creature, with a perfectly simple manner. He has innumerable acquaintances in the school, but only a very few friends. He is amiable with every one, but guards his heart. He is ambitious in a quiet way, and fond of books, and, being brought up in a cultivated home, he can talk more unaffectedly and with a more genuine interest about books than any boy I have ever met. Well, I have done my best, as I say, to make friends with him. I have lent him books; I have tried to make him come and see me; I have talked my best with him, and he has received it all with polite indifference; I can't win his confidence, somehow. I feel that if I were only not in the tutorial relation, it would be easy work. But perhaps I frightened him as a little boy, perhaps I bored him; anyhow the advances are all on my side, and there seems a hedge of shyness through which I cannot break. Sometimes I have thought it is simply a case of "crabbed age and youth," and that I can't put myself sufficiently in line with him. I missed seeing him last night—he was out at some school festivity, and this morning he has gone without a word or a sign. I have made friends a hundred times with a tenth of the trouble, and I suppose it is just because I find this child so difficult to approach that I fret myself over the failure; and all the more because I know in my heart that he is a really congenial nature, and that we do think the same about many things. Of course, most sensible people would not care a brass farthing about such an episode, and would succeed where I have failed, because I think it is the forcing of attentions upon him that this proud young person resents. I must try and comfort myself by thinking that my very capacity for vexing myself over the business is probably the very thing which makes it easy as a rule for me to succeed.

Well, I must turn to my books and my bicycle and my writing for consolation, and to the blessed sense of freedom which luxuriates about my tired brain. But books and art and the beauties of nature, I begin to have a dark suspicion, are of the nature of melancholy consolations for the truer stuff of life—for friendships and loves and dearer things.

I sit writing in my study, the house above me strangely silent. The evening sun lies golden on the lawn and among the apple-trees of my little orchard; but the thought of the sweet time ended lies rather heavy on my heart—the wonder what it all means, why we should have these great hopes and desires, these deep attachments in the short days that God gives us. "What a world it is for sorrow," wrote a wise and tender-hearted old schoolmaster on a day like this; "and how dull it would be if there were no sorrow." I suppose that this is true; but to be near things and yet not to grasp them, to desire and not to attain, and to go down to darkness in the end, like the shadow of a dream—what can heal and sustain one in the grip of such a mood?—Ever yours,

T. B.

UPTON,
Aug. 4, 1904.

MY DEAR HERBERT,—I have just been over to Woodcote; I have had a few days here alone at the end of the half, and was feeling so stupid and lazy this morning that I put a few sandwiches in my pocket and went off on a bicycle for the day. It is only fifteen miles from here, so that I had two or three hours to spend there. You know I was born at Woodcote and lived there till I was ten years old. I don't know the present owner of the Lodge, where we lived; but if I had written and asked to go and see the house, they would have invited me to luncheon, and all my sense of freedom would have gone.

It is thirty years since we left, and I have not been there, near as it is, for twenty years. I did not know how deeply rooted the whole scene was in my heart and memory, but the first sight of the familiar places gave me a very curious thrill, a sort of delicious pain, a yearning for the old days—I can't describe it or analyse it. It seemed somehow as if the old life must be going on there behind the pine-woods if I could only find it; as if I could have peeped over the palings and seen myself going gravely about some childish business in the shrubberies. I find that my memory is curiously accurate in some respects, and curiously at fault in others. The scale is all wrong. What appears to me in memory to be an immense distance, from Woodcote to Dewhurst, for instance, is now reduced to almost nothing; and places which I can see quite accurately in my mind's eye are now so different that I can hardly believe that they were ever like what I recollect of them. Of course the trees have grown immensely; young plantations have become woods, and woods have disappeared. I spent my time in wandering about, retracing the childish walks we used to take, looking at the church, the old houses, the village green, and the mill-pool. One thing came home to me very much. When I was born my father had only been settled at Woodcote for two years; but, as I grew up, it seemed to me we must have lived there for all eternity; now I see that he was only one in a long procession of human visitants who have inhabited and loved the place. Another thing that has gone is the mystery of it all. Then, every road was a little ribbon of familiar ground stretching out to the unknown; all the fields and woods which lay between the roads and paths were wonderful secret places, not to be visited. I find I had no idea of the lie of the ground, and, what is more remarkable, I don't seem ever to have seen the views of the distance with which the place now abounds. I suppose that when one is a small creature, palings and hedges are lofty obstacles; and I suppose also that the little busy eyes are always searching the nearer scene for things to FIND, and do not concern themselves with what is far. The sight of the Lodge itself, with its long white front among the shrubberies and across the pastures was almost too much for me; the years seemed all obliterated in a flash, and I felt as if it was all there unchanged.

I suppose I had a very happy childhood; but I certainly was not in the least conscious of it at the time. I was a very quiet, busy child, with all sorts of small secret pursuits of my own to attend to, to which lessons and social engagements were sad interruptions; but now it seems to me like a golden, unruffled time full of nothing but pleasure. Curiously enough, I can't remember anything but the summer days there; I have no remembrance of rain or cold or winter or leafless trees—except days of snow when the ponds were frozen and there was the wild excitement of skating. My recollections are all of flowers, and roses, and trees in leaf, and hours spent in the garden. In the very hot summer weather my father and mother used to dine out in the garden, and it seems now to me as if they must have done so all the year round; I can remember going to bed, with my window open on to the lawn, and hearing the talk, and the silence, and then the soft clink of the things being removed as I sank into sleep. It is a great mystery, that faculty of the mind for forgetting all the shadows and remembering nothing but the sunlight; it is so deeply rooted in humanity that it is hard not to believe that it means something; one dares to hope that if our individual life continues after death, this instinct—if memory remains—will triumph over the past, even in the case of lives of sordid misery and hopeless pain.

Then, too, one wonders what the strong instinct of permanence means, in creatures that inhabit the world for so short and troubled a space; why instinct should so contradict experience; why human beings have not acquired in the course of centuries a sense of the fleetingness of things. All our instincts seem to speak of permanence; all our experience points to swift and ceaseless change. I cannot fathom it.

As I wandered about Woodcote my thoughts took a sombre tinge, and the lacrimae rerum, the happy days gone, the pleasant groups broken up to meet no more, the old faces departed, the voices that are silent—all these thoughts began to weigh on my mind with a sad bewilderment. One feels so independent, so much the master of one's fate; and yet when one returns to an old home one begins to wonder whether one has any power of choice at all. There is this strange fence of self and identity drawn for me round one tiny body; all that is outside of it has no existence for me apart from consciousness. These are fruitless thoughts, but one cannot always resist them; and why one is here, what these vivid feelings mean, what one's heart-hunger for the sweet world and for beloved people means—all this is dark and secret; and the strong tide bears us on, out of the little harbour of childhood into unknown seas.

Dear Woodcote, dear remembered days, beloved faces and voices of the past, old trees and fields! I cannot tell what you mean and what you are; but I can hardly believe that, if I have a life beyond, it will not somehow comprise you all; for indeed you are my own for ever; you are myself, whatever that self may be.—Ever yours,

T. B.

P.S.—By the way, I want you to do something for me; I want a MAP of your house and of the sitting-rooms. I want to see where you usually sit, to read or write. And more than that, I want a map of the roads and paths round about, with your ordinary walks and strolls marked in red. I don't feel I quite realise the details enough.

SENNICOTTS,
HONEY HILL,
EAST GRINSTEAD,
Aug. 9, 1904.

DEAR HERBERT,—I am making holiday, with the voice of praise and thanksgiving, like the people in the Psalm, and working, oh! how gratefully, at one of my eternal books. Depend upon it, for simple pleasure, there is nothing like writing. I am staying with Bradby, who has taken a cottage in Sussex. He has had his holiday, so that he goes up to town every day; it does not sound very friendly to say that this arrangement exactly suits me, but so it is. I work and write in the morning, walk or bicycle in the afternoon, and then we dine together, and spend peaceful evenings, reading or talking.

But this is not the point. I came in yesterday to tea, saw an unfamiliar hat in the hall, and found to my surprise James Cooper, whom you remember at Eton as a boy. I knew him a little there, and saw a good deal of him at Cambridge; and we have kept up a very fitful correspondence at long intervals ever since.

I am ashamed to confess that I was bored, though I trust to Heaven I did not show it; I had come back from my ride brimming over with ideas, and was in the condition of a person who is holding his breath, dying to blow it all out. Cooper said that he had heard that I was in the neighbourhood, and he had accordingly come over, a considerable distance, to see me. He is in business, and appears to be prospering. We had tea, and there was a good deal to talk about; but Cooper showed no signs of moving, and said at last that he thought he would stay and see Bradby—perhaps dine with us. So we walked about the garden, and I gradually became aware, with regret and misery, that I was in the presence of a bore. Yes, James Cooper is a bore! He had a great deal to say, mostly on subjects with which I was not acquainted. He has become a botanist, and seemed full to the brim of uninteresting information. He stayed till Bradby came, he dined, he talked. At last he decided he must go; but he talked in the hall, he talked in the porch. He pressed us to come over and see him, and it was evidently a great pleasure to him to meet us again. Since his visit I have been pondering deeply. What is one's duty in these matters? How far ought loyalty to old friends to go? I confess that I am somewhat vexed and dissatisfied with myself for not being more simply pleased to see an old comrade—actae non alio rege puertiae, and all that. But what if the old comrade is a bore? What are the claims of friendship on busy men? I have a good many old friends in all parts of England—ought I to use my holidays in touring about to see them? I am inclined to think that I am not bound to do so. But suppose that Cooper goes away, and says to another friend that I am a man who forgets old ties; that he took some trouble to see me, and found me absorbed, and not particularly glad to see him? I hope, indeed, that this was not his impression; but boredom is a subtle thing, and it is difficult to keep it out of one's manner, however religiously one tries to be cheerful. Well, if he DOES feel thus, is he right and am I wrong? His whole life lies on different lines to my own, and though we had much in common in the old pleasant days, we have not much in common now. It is quite possible that he thinks I am a bore; and it is even possible that he is right there too. But, que faire? que penser? I can honestly say that if Cooper wanted my help, my advice, my sympathy, I would give it him without grudging. But is it a part of loyalty that I must desire to see him, and even to be bored by him? I am inclined to think that if I had a simpler, more affectionate nature, I should probably NOT be bored, but that in my gladness at the sight of an old friend and the reviving of old memories, the idea of criticism would die a natural death.

What I have suffered from all my life is making friends too easily. It is so painful to me being with a person who seems to be dull, that I have always instinctively tried to be interested in, and to interest my companion. The result has been—I am making a very barefaced confession—that I have been often supposed to be more friendly than I really am, and to allow a certain claim of loyalty to be established which I could not sincerely sustain.—Ever yours,

T. B.

KNAPSTEAD VICARAGE,
BALDOCK,
Aug. 14, 1904.

MY DEAR HERBERT,—A curious little incident occurred to me yesterday—so curious, so inexplicable, that I cannot refrain from telling it to you, though it has no solution and no moral so far as I can see. I am staying with an old family friend, Duncan by name—you don't know him—who is a parson near Hitchin. We were to have gone for a bicycle ride together, but he was called away on sudden business, and as the only other member of the party is my friend's wife, who is much of an invalid, I went out alone.

I went off through Baldock and Ashwell. And I must interrupt my story for a moment to tell you about the latter. Above a large hamlet of irregularly built and scattered white houses, many of them thatched, most of them picturesque, rises one of the most beautiful, mouldering church towers I have ever seen. It is more like a weather-worn crag-pinnacle than a tower; it is of great height, and the dim and blurred outlines of its arched windows and buttresses communicate a singular grace of underlying form to the broken and fretted stone. I fear that it must before long be restored, if it is to hold together much longer; all I can say is that I am thankful to have seen it in its hour of decay. It is infinitely patient and pathetic. Its solemn, ruinous dignity, its tender grace, make it like some aged and sanctified spirit that has borne calamity and misfortune with a sweet and gentle trust. A little farther on in the village is another extraordinarily beautiful thing. The road, while still almost in the street, passes across a little embankment; and on the left hand you look down into a pit, like a quarry, full of ash-trees, and with a thick undergrowth of bushes and tall plants. From a dozen little excavations leap and bicker crystal rivulets of water, hurrying down stony channels, uniting in a pool, and then moving off, a full-fed stream, among quiet water-meadows. It is one of the sources of the Cam. The water is deliciously cool and clear, running as it does straight off the chalk. No words of mine can do justice to the wonderful purity and peace of the place. I found myself murmuring over those perfect lines of Marvell—you know them?—

"Might a soul bathe there and be clean,
And slake its drought?"

These two sights, the tower and the well-head, put my mind into tune; and I went on my way rejoicing, with that delicate elation of spirit that rarely visits one. Everything I saw had an airy quality, a flavour, an aroma, I know not how to describe it. Now I caught the sunlight on the towering greenness of an ancient elm; now a wide view over flat pastures, with a pool fringed deep in rushes, came in sight; now an old manorial farm held up its lichened chimneys above a row of pollarded elms. I came at last, by lanes and byways, to a silent village that seemed entirely deserted. The men, I suppose, were all working in the fields; the cottage doors stood open; near the little common rose an old high-shouldered church, much overgrown with ivy. The sun lay pleasantly upon its leaded roof, and among the grass-grown graves. I left my bicycle by the porch, and at first could not find an entrance; but at last I discovered that a low, priest's door that led into the chancel, was open. The church had an ancient and holy smell. It was very cool in there out of the sun. I turned into the nave, and wandered about for a few moments, noting the timbered roof, the remains of old frescoes on the walls; the tomb of a knight who lay still and stiff, his head resting on his hand. I read an epitaph or two, with the faint cry of love and grief echoing through the stilted phraseology of the tomb, and then I went back to the altar.

On a broad slab of slate, immediately below the altar steps, lay something dark; I bent down to look at it, and then realised, with a curious sense of horror, that it was a little pool of blood; beside it lay two large jagged stones, also stained with blood, which had dried into a viscous paste upon them. It seemed as if the stoning of some martyr had taken place, and that, the first horrible violence done, the deed had been transferred to the open air. What made it still stranger to me was that in the east window was a rude representation of the stoning of Stephen; and I have since discovered that the church is dedicated to him.

I cannot give you the smallest hint of explanation. Indeed, pondering over it, I cannot conceive of any circumstances which can in any way account for what I saw. I wandered out into the churchyard—for the sight gave me a curious chill of horror—and I could see nothing that could further enlighten me. A few yards beyond stood the rectory, embowered in thickets. It seemed to be deserted; the windows were dark and undraped; no smoke went up from the chimneys. It suddenly appeared to me that I must be the victim of some strange hallucination, So I stepped again within the church to see if my senses had played me false. But no! there were the stones, and the blood beside them.

The sun began to decline to his setting; the shadows lengthened and darkened, as I rode slowly away, with a shadow on my spirit. I felt I had somehow seen a type, a mystery. These incidents do not befall one by chance, and I was sure, in some remote way, that I had looked, as it were, for a moment into a dark avenue of the soul; that I was bidden to think, to ponder. These tokens of violence and death, the blood outpoured, in witness of pain, in the heart of the quiet sanctuary, before the very altar of the God of peace and love. What is it that we do that is like that? What is it that *I* do? I will not tell you how the message shaped itself for me; perhaps you can guess; but it came, it formed itself out of the dark, and in that silent hour a voice called sharply in my spirit.

But I must not end thus. I came home; I told my tale; I found my friend returned. He nodded gravely and wonderingly, and I think he half understood. But his wife was full of curiosity. She made me tell and retell the incident. "Was there no one you could ask?" she said; "I would not have rested till I had solved it." She even bade me tell her the name of the place, but I refused. "Do you mean to say you don't WANT to know?" she said. "No," I said; "I had rather not know." To which, rather petulantly, she said, "Oh, you MEN!" That evening a neighbouring parson, his wife, and daughter, came to dine. I was bidden to tell my story again, and the same scene was re-enacted. "Was there no one you could find to ask?" said the girl. I laughed and said, "I daresay I could have found some one, but I did not want to know. I had rather have my little mystery," I added; and then we men interchanged a nod, while the women looked sharply at each other. "Is it not quite incredible?" my friend's wife said. And the daughter added, "I, for one, will not rest till I have discovered."

That, I suppose, is the difference between the masculine and the feminine mind. You will understand me; but read the story to your wife and daughters, and they will say, "Was there no one he could have asked?" and "I would not rest till I had discovered." Meanwhile I only hope that my maiden's efforts will prove unavailing.—Ever yours,

T. B.

GREENHOWE,
SEDBERGH,
Aug. 21, 1904.

MY DEAR HERBERT,—I suppose I am very early Victorian in my tastes; but I have just been reading Jane Eyre again with intense satisfaction. (I will tell you presently WHY I have been reading it.) I read it first as a boy at Eton, and I must have read it twenty times since. I know that much of it is grotesque, but it seems to me that its grotesqueness is not absurd, any more than the stiff animals and trees or hills in the early

Italian pictures are absurd; one smiles, not contemptuously, but tenderly at it all.

Again, there are two ways of treating a work of art. If a portrait, for instance, is intensely realistic and true to its original, one says, "How lifelike!" If it is widely unlike the original, one can always say, "How symbolical!" Of the first kind of portrait one may say that it brings the man before you; of the latter you may say that the artist has striven to paint the soul rather than the body. Well, I think it is fair to call Jane Eyre symbolical. Some of the people depicted are very true to life. The old, comfortable, good-humoured housekeeper, Mrs. Fairfax; Bessie the nursemaid; Adele, the little French girl, Mr. Rochester's ward; the two Rivers sisters—they are admirable portraits. But Mr. Rochester, the haughty Baroness Ingram of Ingram Park, Miss Ingram, who says to the footman, "Leave that chatter, blockhead, and do my bidding," St. John Rivers, the blue-eyed fanatic—these are caricatures or types, according as you like to view them. To me they are types: characters finely conceived, and only exaggerated because Charlotte Bronte had never mixed with people of that species in ordinary life. But I think that one can see into the souls of these people in spite of the exaggerations of speech and gesture and behaviour which disfigure them. Yet it is not primarily for the character-drawing that I value the book. What attracts me is the romance, the beauty, the poetry of the whole, and a special union of intellectual force, with passion at white heat, which breathes through them. The love scenes have the same strange glow that I always feel in Tennyson's "Come into the garden, Maud," where the pulse of the lover thrills under one's hand with the love that beats from the heart of the world. And then, too, Charlotte Bronte seems to me to have had an incomparable gift of animating a natural scene with vivid human emotions. The frost-bound day, when the still earth holds its breath, when the springs are congealed, and the causeway is black with slippery ice, in that hour when Jane Eyre first sees Mr. Rochester; and again the scene in the summer garden, just before the thunderstorm, when Mr. Rochester calls her to look at the great hawk-moth drinking from the flower chalice. Such scenes have a vitality that makes them as real to me as scenes upon which my own eyes have rested.

Again, I know no writer who has caught the poetry of the hearth like Charlotte Bronte. The evening hours, when the fire leaps in the chimney, and the lamp is lit, and the homeless wind moans outside, and the contented mind possesses its dreams—I know nothing like that in any book.

Indeed, I do not know any books which give me quite the sense of genius that Charlotte Bronte's bring me. I find it difficult to define where the genius lies; but the love which she dares to depict seems to me to have a different quality to any other love; it is the passionate ardour of a pure soul; it embraces body, mind, and heart alike; it is a love that pierces through all disguises, and is the worship of spirit for spirit at the very root of being; such love is not lightly conceived or easily given; it is not born of chance companionship, of fleshly desire, of a craving to share the happiness of a buoyant spirit of sunshine and sweetness; it is rather nurtured in gloom and sadness, it demands a corresponding depth and intensity, it requires to discern in its lover a deep passion for the beauty of virtue. It is one of the triumphs of Jane Eyre that the love she feels for Mr. Rochester pierces through those very superficial vices which would be most abhorrent to the pure nature, if it were not for the certainty that such vice was the disguise and not the essence of the soul. And here lies, I think, the uplifting hopefulness of Jane Eyre, the Christ-like power of recognising the ardent spirit of love behind gross faults of both the animal and the intellectual nature.

I do not know if you ever came across a book—I must send it you if you have not seen it—which moves me and feeds my spirit more than almost any book I know—the Letters and Journals of William Cory. He was a master at Eton, you know, but before our time; and his life was rather a disappointed one; but he had that remarkable union of qualities which I think is very rare—hard intellectual force with passionate tenderness. I suppose that, as far as mental ability went, he was one of the very foremost men of his day. He had a faultless memory, great clearness and vigour of thought, and perfect lucidity of expression. But he valued these gifts very little in comparison with feeling, which was his real life. It always interests me deeply to find that he had the same opinion of Charlotte Bronte that I hold; and indeed I have always thought that, allowing for a difference of nationality, he was very much the kind of man whom she depicted in Villette as Paul Emmanuel.

Personality is, after all, the ultimate foundation of art, and I think that what I value most of all in Charlotte Bronte's books is the revelation of herself that they afford. The shy, frail, indomitable, ardent creature, inured to poverty and hardness, without illusions, without material temptations, but all aglow with the sacred fire—such is the character that here emerges. Charlotte Bronte as a writer seems to me like a burning-glass which concentrates on one intense point the fiercest fire of the soul. I would humbly believe that there is much of this spirit in the world, but that it seldom co-exists with the artistic power, the intellectual force, that enables it to express itself.

And now I will tell you what has made me take up Jane Eyre again at this time. I was bicycling a day or two ago in a secluded valley under the purple heights of Ingleboro'. I passed a little village, with a big building standing by a stream below the road, called Lowood. It came into my head as a pleasant thought that some place like this might have been the scene of the schooldays of Jane Eyre; but I thought no more of it, till a little while after I saw a tablet in the wall of a house by the wayside. I dismounted, and behold! it was the very place, the very building where Charlotte Bronte spent her schooldays. It was a low, humble building, now divided into cottages. But you can still see the windows of the dormitory, the little kitchen garden, the brawling stream, the path across the meadows, and, beyond all, the long line of the moor. In a house just opposite was a portrait of Mr. Brocklehurst himself (his real name was Carus-Wilson), so sternly, and I expect unjustly, gibbetted in the book. That was a very sacred hour for me. I thought of Miss Temple and Helen Burns; I thought of the cold, the privation, the rigour of that comfortless place. But I felt that it was good to be there. I drew nearer in that hour to the unquenched spirit that battled so gloriously with life and with its worst terrors and sorrows, and that wrote so firmly and truly its pure hopes and immortal dreams....—Ever yours,

T. B.

ASHFIELD,
SETTLE,
Aug. 27, 1904.

DEAR HERBERT,—You ask me to send you out some novels, and you have put me in a difficulty. It seems hardly worth while sending out books which will just be read once or twice in a lazy mood and then thrown aside; yet I can find no others. It seems to me that our novelists are at the present moment affected by the same wave which seems to be passing over the whole of our national life; we have in every department a large number of almost first-rate people, men of talent and ability; but very few geniuses, very few people of undisputed pre-eminence. In literature this is particularly the case; poets, historians, essayists, dramatists, novelists; there are so many that reach a high level of accomplishment, and do excellent work; but there are no giants, or they are very small ones. Personally, I do not read a great many novels; and I find myself tending to revert again and again to my old favourites.

Of course there are some CONSPICUOUS novelists. There is George Meredith, though he has now almost ceased to write; to speak candidly, though I recognise his genius, his creative power, his noble and subtle conception of character, yet I do not feel the reality of his books; or rather I feel that the reality is there, but disguised from me by a veil—a dim and rich veil, it is true—which is hung between me and the scene. The veil is George Meredith's personality. I confess that it is a dignified personality enough, the spirit of a grand seigneur. But I feel in reading his books as if I were staying with a magnificent person in a stately house; but that, when I wanted to go about and look at things for myself, my host, with splendid urbanity, insisted on accompanying me, pointed out objects that interested himself, and translated the remarks of the guests and the other people who appeared upon the scene into his own peculiar diction. The characters do not talk as I think they would have talked, but as George Meredith would have talked under the given circumstances. There is no repose about his books; there is a sense not only of intellectual but actually of moral effort about reading them; and further, I do not like the style; it is highly mannerised, and permeated, so to speak, with a kind of rich perfume, a perfume which stupefies rather than enlivens. Even when the characters are making what are evidently to them perfectly natural and straightforward remarks, I do not feel sure what they mean; and I suffer from paroxysms of rage as I read, because I feel that I cannot get at what is there without a mental agility which seems to me unnecessarily fatiguing. A novel ought to be like a walk; George Meredith makes it into an obstacle race.

Then, again, Henry James is an indubitably great writer; though you amused me once by saying that you felt you really had not time to read his later books. Well, for myself, I confess that his earlier books, such as Roderick Hudson and the Portrait of a Lady, are books that I recur to again and again. They are perfectly proportioned and admirably lucid. If they have a fault, and I do not readily admit it, it is that the characters are not quite full-blooded enough. Still, there is quite enough of what is called "virility" about in literature; and it is refreshing to find oneself in the company of people who preserve at all events the conventional decencies of life. But Henry James has in his later books taken a new departure; he is infinitely subtle and extraordinarily delicate; but he is obscure where he used to be lucid, and his characters now talk in so allusive and birdlike a way, hop so briskly from twig to twig, that one cannot keep the connection in one's mind. He seems to be so afraid of anything that is obvious or plain-spoken, that his art conceals not art but nature. I declare that in his conversations I have not unfrequently to reckon back to see who has got the ball; then, too, those long, closely printed pages, such as one sees in The Wings of a Dove, without paragraphs, without breathing places, pages of minute and refined analysis—there is a high intellectual pleasure in reading them, but there is a mental strain as well. It is as though one wandered in tortuous passages, full of beautiful and curious things, without ever reaching the rooms of the house. What I want, in a work of imagination, is to step as simply as possible into the presence of an emotion, the white heat of a situation. With Henry James I do not feel certain what the situation is. At the same time his books are full of fine things; he has learnt a splendid use of metaphor, when the whole page seems, as it were, stained with some poetical thought, as though one had shut a fruit into the book, and its juice had tinted the whole of a page. But that is not sufficient; and I confess I close one of his later volumes in a condition of admiring mystification. I do not know what it has all been about; the characters have appeared, have nodded and smiled inscrutably, have let fall sentences which seem like sparkling fragments of remarks; I feel that there is a great conception behind, but I am still in the dark as to what it is.

There are two or three other authors whose books I read with interest. One of these is John Oliver Hobbes. Her books do not seem to me to be exactly natural; it is all of the nature of a scenic display. But there is abundance of nobility and even of passion; and the style is original, nervous, and full of fine aphorisms. There is a feeling of high and chivalrous courage about her characters; they breathe perhaps too lofty an air, and are, if anything, too true to themselves. But it is a dignified romance, rather mediaeval than modern, and penetrated with a pungent aromatic humour which has a quality of its own.

Mrs. Humphry Ward is another writer whose books I always read. I am constantly aware of a great conscientiousness in the background. The scenery, the people, are all studied with the most sedulous and patient care; but I somehow feel, at all events in the earlier works, that the moral attitude of the writer, a kind of Puritan agnosticism, interferes with the humanity of the books; they seem to me to be as saturated with principle as Miss Yonge's books, written from a very different standpoint, were. I feel that I am not to be allowed my own preferences, and that to enjoy the books I must be in line with the authoress. Mrs. Ward's novels, in fact, seem to me the high-water mark of what great talent, patient observation, and faithful work can do; but the light does not quite shine through. Yet it is only just to say that every book Mrs. Ward writes seems an improvement on the last. There is a wider, larger, freer conception of life; more reality, more humanity, as well as more artistic handling; and they are worth careful reading; I shall certainly include one or two in my consignment.

George Moore seems to me to be one of the best writers on the stage. Esther Waters, Evelyn Innes, and Sister Theresa, are books of the highest quality. I have a sense in these books of absolute reality. I may think the words and deeds of the characters mysterious, surprising, and even sometimes disgusting; but they surprise and disgust me just as the anomalies of human beings affect me. I may not like them, but I do not question the fact that the characters spoke and behaved as they are supposed to behave. Moreover, Evelyn Innes and Sister Theresa are written in a style of matchless lucidity and precision; they have passages of high poetry. Old Mr. Innes, with his tiresome preoccupations, his pedantic taste, his mediaeval musical instruments, affects me exactly as an unrelenting idealist does in actual life. The mystical Ulick has a profound charm; the Sisters in the convent, all preoccupied with the same or similar ideas, have each a perfectly distinct individuality. Evelyn herself, even with all her frank and unashamed sensuality, is a deeply attractive figure; and I know no books which so render the evasive charm of the cloistered life. But George Moore has two grave faults; he is sometimes vulgar and he is sometimes brutal. Evelyn's worldly lover is a man who makes one's flesh creep, and yet one feels he is intended to represent the fascination of the world. Then it does not seem to me to be true realism to depict scenes of frank animalism. Such things may occur; but the actors in such a carnival could not speak of them, even to each other; it may be prudish, but I cannot help feeling that one ought not to have represented in a book what could not be repeated in conversation or depicted in a picture. One may be plain-spoken enough in art, but one ought not to have the feeling that one would be ashamed, in certain passages, to catch the author's eye.

If it were not for these lapses, I should put George Moore at the head of all contemporary novelists; and I am not sure that I do not do so as it is. Do give them another trial; I always thought you were too easily discouraged in your attempt to grapple with his books; probably my admiration for them only aroused your critical sense; and I admit that there is much to criticise.

Then there is another writer, lately dead, alas, whose books I used to read with absorbing interest, George Gissing. They had, when he treated of his own peculiar stratum, the same quality of hard reality which I value most of all in a work of fiction. The actors were not so much vulgar as underbred; their ambitions and tastes were often deplorable. But one felt that they were real people. The wall of the suburban villa was gently removed, and the life was before your eyes. The moment he strayed from that milieu, the books became fantastic and unreal. But in the last two books, By the Ionian Sea and the Papers of Henry Rycroft, Gissing stepped into a new province, and produced exquisitely beautiful and poetical idealistic literature.

Thomas Hardy is a poetical writer. But his rustic life, dreamy, melancholy, and beautiful as it is, with the wind blowing fragrant out of the heart of the wood, or the rain falling on the down, seems to me to be no more real than the scenes in As You Like It or The Tempest. The figures are actors playing a part. And then there is through his books so strong a note of sex, and people under the influence of passion seem to me to behave in so incomprehensible a way, in a manner so foreign to my own experience, that though I would not deny the truth of the picture, I would say that it is untrue for me, and therefore unmeaning.

I have never fallen under the sway of Rudyard Kipling. Whenever I read his stories I feel myself for the time in the grip of a strong mind, and it becomes a species of intoxication. But I am naturally sober by inclination, and though I can unreservedly admire the strength, the vigour, the splendid imaginativeness of his conceptions, yet the whole note of character is distasteful to me. I don't like his male men; I should dislike them and be ill at ease with them in real life, and I am ill at ease with them in his books. This is purely a matter of taste; and as to the animal stories, terrifically clever as they are, they appear to me to be no more true to life than Landseer's pictures of dogs holding a coroner's inquest or smoking pipes. The only book of his that I re-read is The Light that Failed, for its abundant vitality and tragicalness; but the same temperamental repugnance overcomes me even there.

For pure imagination I should always fly to a book by H. G. Wells. He has that extraordinary power of imagining the impossible, and working it out in a hard literal way which is absolutely convincing. But he is a teller of tales and not a dramatist.

Well, you will be tired of all these fussy appreciations. But what one seems to miss nowadays is the presence of a writer of superlative lucidity and humanity, for whose books one waits with avidity, and orders them beforehand, as soon as they are announced. For one thing, most people seem to me to write too much. The moment a real success is scored, the temptation, no doubt adroitly whispered by publishers, to produce a similar book on similar lines, becomes very strong. Few living writers are above the need for earning money; but even that would not spoil a genius if we had him.

These writers whom I have mentioned seem to me all like little bubbling rivulets, each with a motion, a grace, a character of its own. But what one craves for is a river deep and wide, for some one, with a great flood of humanity like Scott, or with a leaping cataract of irrepressible humour like Dickens, or with a core of white-hot passion like Charlotte Bronte, or a store of brave and wholesome gaiety and zest, such as Stevenson showed.

Well, we must wait and hope. Meanwhile I will write to my great book-taster; one of the few men alive with great literary vitality, who has never indulged the temptation to write, and has never written a line. I will show him the manner of man you are, and a box of bright volumes shall be packed for you. The one condition is that you shall write me in return a sheet of similar appreciations. The only thing is to know what one likes, and strike out a line for oneself; the rest is mere sheep-like grazing—forty feeding like one.—Ever yours,

T. B.

ASHFIELD,
SETTLE,
Sept. 4, 1904.

DEAR HERBERT,—I have been reading FitzGerald's pretty essay Euphranor. It is Platonic both in form and treatment, but I never feel that it is wholly successful. Most of the people who express admiration for it know nothing of the essay except a delicious passage at the end, like a draught of fragrant wine, about the gowned figures evaporating into the twilight, and the nightingale heard among the flowering chestnuts of Jesus. But the talk itself is discursive and somewhat pompous. However, it is not of that that I wish to speak, it is rather of the passage from Digby's Godefridus which is read aloud by the narrator, which sets out to analyse the joyful and generous temperament of Youth. "They [the young] are easily put to Shame" (so runs the script), "for they have no resources to set aside the precepts which they have learned; and they have lofty souls, for they have never been disgraced or brought low, and they are unacquainted with Necessity; they prefer Honour to Advantage, Virtue to Expediency; for they live by Affection rather than by Reason, and Reason is concerned with Expediency, but Affection with Honour."

All very beautiful and noble, no doubt; but is it real? was I, were you, creatures of this make? Could these fine things have been truthfully said of us? Perhaps you may think it of yourself, but I can only regretfully say that I do not recognise it.

My boyhood and youth were, it seems to me, very faulty things. My age is faulty still, more's the pity. But without any vain conceit, and with all the humility which is given by a knowledge of weakness, I can honestly say that in particular points I have improved a little. I am not generous or noble-hearted now; but I have not lost these qualities, for I never had them. As a boy and a young man I distinctly preferred Advantage to Honour; I was the prey of Expediency, and seldom gave Virtue a thought. But since I have known more of men, I have come to know that these fine powers, Honour and Virtue, do bloom in some men's souls, and in the hearts of many women. I have perceived their fragrance; I have seen Honour raise its glowing face like a rose, and Virtue droop its head like a pure snowdrop; and I hope that some day, as in an early day of spring, I may find some such tender green thing budding in the ugly soil of my own poor spirit.

Life would be a feeble business if it were otherwise; but the one ray of hope is not that one steadily declines in brightness from those early days, but that one may learn by admiration the beauty of the great qualities one never had by instinct.

I see myself as a boy, greedy, mean-spirited, selfish, dull. I see myself as a young man, vain, irritable, self-absorbed, unbalanced. I have not eradicated these weeds; but I have learnt to believe in beauty and honour, even in Truth....—Ever yours,

T. B.

MONK'S ORCHARD,
UPTON,
Sept. 13, 1904.

DEAR HERBERT,—I have just come back after a long, vague holiday, feeling well and keen about my work. The boys are not back yet, and I have returned to put things ready for next half. But my serene mood has received a shock this morning.

I wonder if you ever get disagreeable letters? I suppose that a schoolmaster is peculiarly liable to receive them. The sort of letter I mean is this. I come down to breakfast in good spirits; I pick up a letter and open it, and, all of a sudden, it is as if a snake slipped out and bit me. I close it and put it away, thinking I will read it later; there it lies close by my plate, and takes away the taste of food, and blots the sunshine. I take it upstairs, saying that it will want consideration. I finish my other letters, and then I take it out again. Out comes the snake again with a warning hiss; but I resist temptation this time, read it through, and sit staring out of the window. A disagreeable letter from a disagreeable man, containing anxious information, of a kind that I cannot really test. What is the best way to deal with it? I know by experience; answer it at once, as dispassionately as one can; extract from it the few grains of probable truth it holds, and keep them in mind for possible future use; then deliberately try and forget all about it. I know now by experience that the painful impression will gradually fade, and, meanwhile, one must try to interpret the whole matter rightly. What is there in one's conduct which needs the check? Is it that one grows confident and careless? Probably! But the wholesome thing to do is to deal with it at once; otherwise it means anxious and feverish hours, when one composes a long and epigrammatic answer, point by point. The letter is over-stated, gossipy, malicious; if one lets it soak into the mind, it makes one suspicious of every one, miserable, cowardly. It is useless in the first hours, when the sting is yet tingling, to remind oneself philosophically that the suggestion is exaggerated and malignant; one does not get any comfort that way. No, the only thing is to plunge into detail, to work, to read—anything to recover the tone of the mind.

It is a comfort to write to you about it, for to-day I am in the sore and disquieted condition which is just as unreal and useless as though I were treating the matter with indifference. Indifference indeed would be criminal, but morbidity is nearly as bad.

I once saw a very dramatic thing take place in church. It was in a town parish near my old home. The clergyman was a friend of mine, a wonderfully calm and tranquil person. He went up to the pulpit while a hymn was being sung. When the hymn concluded, he did not give out his text, but remained for a long time silent, so long that I thought he was feeling ill; the silence became breathless, and the attention of every one in the church became rivetted on the pulpit. Then he slowly took up a letter from the cushion, and said in a low, clear voice: "A fortnight ago I found, on entering the pulpit, a letter addressed to me in an unknown hand; I took it out and read it afterwards; it was anonymous, and its contents were scandalous. Last Sunday I found another, which I burnt unread. To-day there is another, which I do not intend to read"—he tore the letter across as he said the words, in the sight of the congregation—"and I give notice that, if any further communications of the kind reach me, I shall put the matter into the hands of the police. I am willing to receive, if necessary, verbal communications on such subjects, though I do not think that any good purpose can be served by them. But to make vague and libellous accusations against members of the congregation in this way is cowardly, dishonourable, and un-Christian. I have a strong suspicion"—he looked steadily down the church—"of the quarter from which these letters emanate; and I solemnly warn the writer that, if I have to take action in the matter, I shall take measures to make that action effective."

I never saw a thing better done; it was said without apparent excitement or agitation; he presently gave out his text and preached as usual. It seemed to me a supremely admirable way of dealing with the situation. Need I add that he was practical enough to take the pieces of the letter away with him?

I once received an anonymous letter, not about myself, but about a friend. I took it to a celebrated lawyer, and we discovered the right way to deal with it. I remember that, when we had finished, he took up the letter—a really vile document—and said musingly: "I have often wondered what the pleasure of sending such things consists in! I always fancy the sender taking out his watch, and saying, with malicious glee, 'I suppose so-and-so will be receiving my letter about now!' It must be a perverted sense of power, I think."

I said, "Yes, and don't you think that there is also something of the pleasure of saying 'Bo' to a goose?" The great man smiled, and said, "Perhaps."

Well, I must try to forget, but I don't know anything that so takes the courage and the cheerfulness out of one's mind as one of these secret, dastardly things. My letter this morning was not anonymous; but it was nearly as bad, because it was impossible to use or to rely upon the information; and it was, moreover, profoundly disquieting.

Tell me what you think! I suppose it is good for one to know how weak one's armour is and how vulnerable is one's feeble self.—Ever yours,

T. B.

UPTON,
Sept. 20, 1904.

DEAR HERBERT,—I have been reading lately, not for the first time, but with increased interest, the Memoir of Mark Pattison. It was, you will remember, dictated by himself towards the end of his life, and published after his death with a few omissions. It was not favourably received, and was called cowardly, cynical, bitter, a "cry in the dark," treacherous, and so forth. It is very difficult not to be influenced by current opinion in one's view of a book; one comes to it prepared to find certain characteristics, and it is difficult to detach one's mind sufficiently to approach a much-reviewed volume with perfect frankness. But I have read the book several times, and my admiration for it increases. It does not reveal a generous or particularly attractive character, and there are certain episodes in it which are undoubtedly painful. But it is essentially a just, courageous, and candid book. He is very hard on other people, and deals hard knocks. He shows very clearly that he was deficient in tolerance and sympathy, but he is quite as severe on himself. What I value in the book is its absolute sincerity. He does not attempt to draw an ideal picture of his own life and character at the expense of other people. One sees him develop from the shy, gauche, immature boy into the mature, secluded, crabbed, ungracious student. If he had adopted a pose he might have sketched his own life in beautiful subdued colours; he might have made himself out as misrepresented and misunderstood. He does none of these things. He shows clearly that the disasters of his life were quite as much due to his own temperamental mistakes as to the machinations of others. He has no illusions about himself, and he does not desire that his readers should have any. The sadness of the book comes from his failure, or rather his constitutional inability, to see other people whole. After all, our appreciations for other people are of the nature of a sum. There is a certain amount of addition and subtraction to be done; the point is whether the sum total is to the credit of the person concerned. But with Mark Pattison the process of subtraction was more congenial than the process of addition. He saw and felt the weakness of those who surrounded him so keenly that he did not do justice to their good qualities. This comes out very clearly when he deals with Newman and Pusey. Pattison was a member for a time of the Tractarian set, but he must have been always at heart a Liberal and a Rationalist, and the spell which Newman temporarily cast over him appeared to him in after life to have been a kind of ugly hypnotism, to which he had limply submitted. Certainly the diary which he quotes concerning his own part in the Tractarian movement, the conversations to which he listened, the morbid frame of mind to which he succumbed are deplorable reading. Indeed the reminiscences of Newman's conversation in particular, the pedantry, the hankering after miracles, the narrowness of view, are an extraordinary testimony to the charm with which Newman must have invested all he did or said. Pattison is even more severe on Pusey, and charges him with having betrayed a secret which he had confided to him in confession. It does not seem to occur to Pattison to consider whether he did not himself mention the fact, whatever it was, to some other friend.

On the other hand the book reveals an extraordinary intellectual ideal. It holds up a standard for the student which is profoundly impressive; and I know no other book which displays in a more single-minded and sincere way the passionate desire of the savant for wide, deep, and perfect knowledge, which is to be untainted by any admixture of personal ambition. Indeed, Pattison speaks of literary ambition as being for the student not an amiable weakness, but a defiling and polluting sin.

Of course it is natural to feel that there is a certain selfish aridity about such a point of view. The results of Mark Pattison's devotion are hardly commensurate with his earnestness. He worked on a system which hardly permitted him to put the results at the disposal of others; but there is at the same time something which is both dignified and stately in the idea of the lonely, laborious life, without hope and without reward, sustained only by the pursuit of an impossible perfection.

It is not, however, as if this was all that Mark Pattison did. He was a great intellectual factor at Oxford, especially in early days; in later days he was a venerable and splendid monument. But as tutor of his college, before his great disappointment—his failure to be elected to the Rectorship—he evidently lived a highly practical and useful life. There is something disarming about the naive way in which he records that he became aware that he was the possessor of a certain magnetic influence to which gradually every one in the place, including the old Rector himself, submitted.

The story of his failure to be elected Rector is deeply pathetic. Pattison reveals with terrible realism the dingy and sordid intrigues which put an unworthy man in the place which he himself had earned. But it may be doubted whether there was so much malignity about the whole matter as he thought; and, at all events, it may be said that men do not commonly make enemies without reason. It does not seem to occur to him to question whether his own conduct and his own remarks may not have led to the unhappy situation; and indeed, if he spoke of his colleagues in his lifetime with the same acrimony with which his posthumous book speaks of them, the mystery is adequately explained.

His depression and collapse, which he so mercilessly chronicles, after the disaster, do not appear to me to be cowardly. He was an over-worked, over-strained man, with a strong vein of morbidity in his constitution; and to have the great prize of a headship, which was the goal of his dearest hopes, put suddenly and evidently quite unexpectedly in his hands, and then in so unforeseen a manner torn away, must have been a terrible and unmanning catastrophe. What is ungenerous is that he did not more tenderly realise that eventually it all turned out for the best. He recognises the fact somewhat grudgingly. Yet he was disengaged by the shock from professional life. He gained bodily strength and vigour by the change; he began his work of research; and then, just at the time when his ideal was consolidated, the Rectorship came to him—when it might have seemed that by his conduct he had forfeited all hopes of it.

In another respect the book is admirable. Mark Pattison attained high and deserved literary distinction; but there is no hint of complacency on this subject, rather, indeed, the reverse; for he confesses that success had upon him no effect but to humiliate him by the consideration that the completed work might have been so much better both in conception and execution than it actually was.

I feel, on closing the book, a great admiration for the man, mingled with infinite pity for the miseries which his own temperament inflicted on him; it gives me, too, a high intellectual stimulus; it makes me realise the nobility and the beauty of knowledge, the greatness of the intellectual life. One may regret that in Pattison's case this was not mingled with more practical power, more sympathy, more desire to help rather than to pursue. But here, again, one cannot have everything, and the life presents a fine protest against materialism, against the desire of recognition, against illiberal and retrograde views of thought. Here was a great and lonely figure haunted by a dream which few of those about him could understand, and with which hardly any could sympathise. He writes pathetically: "I am fairly entitled to say that, since the year 1851, I have lived wholly for study. There can be no vanity in making this confession, for, strange to say, in a university ostensibly endowed for the cultivation of science and letters, such a life is hardly regarded as a creditable one."

The practical effect of such a book on me is to make me realise the high virtue of thoroughness. It is not wholly encouraging, because at a place like this one must do a good deal of one's work sloppily and sketchily; but it makes me ashamed of my sketchiness; I make good resolutions to get up my subjects better, and, even if I know that I shall relapse, something will have been gained. But that is a side-issue. The true gain is to have been confronted with a real man, to have looked into the depth of his spirit, to realise differences of temperament, to be initiated into a high and noble ambition. And at the same time, alas! to learn by his failures to value tact and sympathy and generosity still more; and to learn that noble purpose is ineffective if it is secluded; to try resolutely to see the strong points of other workers, rather than their feeblenesses; and to end by feeling that we have all of us abundant need to forgive and to be forgiven—Ever yours,

T. B.

UPTON,
Sept. 26, 1904.

DEAR HERBERT,—I am much exercised in my mind about school sermons. It seems to me that we ought to make more of them than we do. We have our sermons here, very wisely, I think, at the evening service. The boys are more alert, the preacher is presumably in a more genial mood, the chapel is warm and brightly lighted, the music has had a comforting and stimulating effect upon the mind; it is exactly the time when the boys are ready and disposed to be interested in themselves, their lives and characters; they are hopeful, serious, ardent. The iron is hot, and it is just the moment to strike.

Well, it seems to me that the opportunity is often missed. In the first place, all the clerical members of the staff are asked to preach in turn—"given a mount," as the boys say. The headmaster preaches once a month, and a certain number of outside preachers, old Uptonians, local clergy, and others are imported.

Now the first point that strikes me is that to suppose that every clergyman is ipso facto capable of preaching at all is a great mistake. I suppose that every thoughtful Christian must have enough materials for a few sermons; there must be some aspects of truth that come home to every individual in a striking manner, some lessons of character which he has learnt. But he need not necessarily have the art of expressing himself in a penetrating and incisive way. It seems to me a mistaken sort of conscientiousness which makes it necessary for every preacher to compose his own sermons. I do not see why the sermons of great preachers should not frankly be read; one hears a dull sermon by a tired man on a subject of which Newman has treated with exquisite lucidity and feeling in one of his parochial sermons. Why is it better to hear tedious considerations on the same point expressed in a commonplace way than to listen to the words of a master of the art, and one too who saw, like Newman, very deep into the human heart? I would have a man frankly say at the beginning of his sermon that he had been thinking about a particular point, and that he was going to read one of Newman's sermons on the subject. Then, if any passage was obscure or compressed, he might explain it a little.

Again, I want more homeliness, more simplicity, more directness in sermons; and so few people seem to be aware that these qualities of expression are not only the result of being a homely, simple, and direct character, but are a matter of long practice and careful art.

Then, again, I want sermons to be more shrewd and incisive. Holiness, saintliness, and piety are virtues which are foreign to the character of boys. If any proof of it is needed, it is only too true that if a boy applies any of the three adjectives holy, saintly, or pious to a person, it is not intended to be a compliment. The words in their mouths imply sanctimonious pretension, and a certain Pharisaical and even hypocritical scrupulousness. It is a great mistake to overlook this fact; I do not mean that a preacher should not attempt to praise these virtues, but if he does, he ought to be able to translate his thoughts into language which will approve itself to boys; he ought to be able to make it clear that such qualities are not inconsistent with manliness, humour, and kindliness. A school preacher ought to be able to indulge a vein of gentle satire; he ought to be able to make boys ashamed of their absurd conventionalism; he ought to give the impression that because he is a Christian he is none the less a man of the world in the right sense. He ought not to uphold what, for want of a better word, I will call a feminine religion, a religion of sainted choir-boys and exemplary death-beds. A boy does not want to be gentle, meek, and mild, and I fear I cannot say that it is to be desired that he should. But if a man is shrewd and even humorous first, he can lift his audience into purer and higher regions afterwards; and he will then be listened to, because his hearers will feel that the qualities they most admire—strength, keenness, good humour—need not be left behind at the threshold of the Christian life, but may be used and practised in the higher regions.

Then, too, I think that there is a sad want of variety. How rarely does one hear a biographical sermon; and yet biography is one of the things to which almost all boys will listen spellbound. I wish that a preacher would sometimes just tell the story of some gallant Christian life, showing the boys that they too may live such lives if they have the will. Preachers dwell far too much on the side of self-sacrifice and self-abnegation. Those, it seems to me, are much more mature ideals. I wish that they would dwell more upon the enjoyment, the interest, the amusement of being good in a vigorous way.

What has roused these thoughts in me are two sermons I have lately heard here. On Sunday week a great preacher came here, and spoke with extraordinary force and sense upon the benefits to be derived from making the most of chapel services. I never heard the thing better done. He gave the simplest motives for doing it. He said that we all believed in goodness in our hearts, and that a service, if we came to it in the right way, was a means of hammering goodness in. That it was a good thing that chapel services were compulsory, because if they were optional, a great many boys would stay away out of pure laziness, and lose much good thereby. And as they were compulsory, we had better make the most we could of them. He went on to speak of attention, of posture, and so forth. There are a certain number of big boys here, who have an offensive habit of putting their heads down upon their arms on the book-board during a sermon, and courting sleep. The preacher made a pause at this point, and said that it was, of course, true that an attitude of extreme devotion did not always mean a corresponding seriousness of mind. There was a faint ripple of mirth at this, and then, one by one, the boys who were engaged in attempting to sleep raised themselves slowly up in a sheepish manner, trying to look as if they were only altering their position naturally. It was intensely ludicrous; but so good for the offenders! And then the preacher rose into a higher vein, and said how the thought of the school chapel would come back to the boys in distant days; that the careless would wish in vain that they had found the peace of Christ there, and that those who had worshipped in spirit and truth would be thankful that it had been so. And then he drew a little picture of a manly, pure, and kind ideal of a boy's life in words that made all hearts go out to him. Boys are heedless creatures; but I am sure that many of them, for a day or two at all events, tried to live a better life in the spirit of that strong and simple message.

Well, yesterday we had a man of a very different sort; earnest enough and high-minded, I am sure, but he seemed to have forgotten, if he had ever known, what a boy's heart and mind were like. The sermon was devoted to imploring boys to take Orders, and he drew a dismal picture of the sacrifices the step entailed, and depicted, in a singularly unattractive vein, the life of a city curate. Now the only way to make the thought of such a life appeal to boys is to indicate the bravery, the interest of it all, the certainty that you are helping human beings, the enjoyment which always attaches to human relationship.

The result was, I confess, extremely depressing. He made a fervent appeal at the end; "The call," he said, "comes to you now and to-day." I watched from my stall with, I am sorry to say, immense amusement, the proceedings of a great, burly, red-faced boy, a prominent football player, and a very decent sort of fellow. He had fallen asleep early in the discourse; and at this urgent invitation, he opened one eye and cast it upon the preacher with a serene and contented air. Finding that the call did not appear to him to be particularly imperative, he slowly closed it again, and, with a good-tempered sigh, addressed himself once more to repose. I laughed secretly, hoping the preacher did not observe his hearer.

But, seriously, it seemed to me a lamentable waste of opportunities. The Sunday evening service is the one time in the week when there is a chance of putting religion before the boys in a beautiful light. Most of them desire to be good, I think; their half-formed wishes, their faltering hopes, their feeble desires, ought to be tenderly met, and lifted, and encouraged. At times, too, a stern morality ought to be preached and enforced; wilful transgression ought to be held up in a terrible light. I do not really mind how it is done, but the heart ought somehow to be stirred and awakened. There is room for denunciation and there is room for encouragement. Best of all is a due admixture of both; if sin can be shown in its true colours, if the darkness, the horror, the misery of the vicious life can be displayed, and the spirit then pointed to the true and right path, the most is done that can be done.

But we grow so miserably stereotyped and mannerised. My cautious colleagues are dreadfully afraid of anything which they call revivalistic, and, indeed, of anything which is unconventional. I should like to see the Sunday sermon made one of the most stirring events of the week, as Arnold made it at Rugby. I should like preachers to be selected with the utmost care, and told beforehand what they were to preach about. No instruction is wanted in a school chapel—the boys get plenty of that in their Divinity lessons. What is wanted is that the heart should be touched, and that faint strivings after purity and goodness should be enforced and helped. To give the spirit wings, that ought to be the object. But so often we have to listen to a conscientious discourse, in which the preacher, after saying that the scene in which the narrative is laid is too well known to need description, proceeds to paint an ugly picture out of The Land and the Book or Farrar's Life of Christ. The story is then tediously related, and we end by a few ethical considerations, taken out of the footnotes of the Cambridge Bible for Schools or Homiletical Hints, which make even the most ardent Christian feel that after all the pursuit of perfection is a very dreary business.

But a brave, wise-hearted, and simple man, speaking from the heart to the heart, not as one who has attained to a standard of impossible perfection, but as an elder pilgrim, a little older, a little stronger, a little farther on the way—what cannot such an one do to set feeble feet on the path, and turn souls to the light? Boys are often pathetically anxious to be good; but they are creatures of impulse, and what they need is to feel that goodness is interesting, beautiful, and desirable.... Ever yours,

T. B.

UPTON,
Oct. 5, 1904.

DEAR HERBERT,—It is autumn now with us, the sweetest season of the year to a polar bear like myself. Of course, Spring is ravishingly, enchantingly beautiful, but she brings a languor with her, and there are the hot months to be lived through, treading close on her heels. But now the summer is over and done; the long firelit evenings are coming, and, as if to console one for the loss of summer beauty, the whole world blazes out into a rich funeral pomp. I walked to-day with a friend to a place not far away, a great, moated house in a big, ancient park. We left the town, held on through the wretched gradations of suburbanity, and then, a few hundred yards from the business-like, treeless high-road, the coverts came in sight. There is always a dim mystery about a close-set wood showing its front across the fields. It always seems to me like a silent battalion guarding some secret thing. We left the high-road and soon were in the wood—the dripping woodways, all strewn with ruinous gold, opening to right and left; and soon the roofs and towers of the big house—Puginesque Gothic, I must tell you—came in sight. But those early builders of the romantic revival, though they loved stucco and shallow niches, had somehow a sense of mass. It pleases me to know that the great Sir Walter himself had a hand in the building of this very house, planned the barbican and the water-gate. All round the house lies a broad moat of black water, full of innumerable carp. The place was breathlessly still; only the sharp melancholy cries of water-birds and the distant booming of guns broke the silence. The water was all sprinkled with golden leaves, that made a close carpet round the sluices; the high elms were powdered with gold; the chestnuts showed a rustier red. A silent gardener, raking leaves with ancient leisureliness, was the only sign of life—he might have been a spirit for all the sound he made; while the big house blinked across the rich clumps of Michaelmas daisies, and the dark windows showed a flicker of fire darting upon the walls. Everything seemed mournful, yet contented, dying serenely and tranquilly, with a great and noble dignity. I wish I could put into words the sweet solemnity, the satisfying gravity of the scene; it was like the sight of a beautiful aged face that testifies to an inner spirit which has learnt patience, tenderness, and trustfulness from experience, and is making ready, without fear or anxiety, for the last voyage.

I say gratefully that this is one of the benefits of growing older, that these beautiful things seem to speak more and more instantly to the mind. Perhaps the faculty of eager enjoyment is somewhat blunted; but the appeal, the sweetness, the pathos, the mystery of the world, as life goes on, fall far oftener and with far more of a magical spell upon the heart.

We walked for a while by a bridge, where the stream out of the moat ran hoarsely, choked with drift, in its narrow walls. That melancholy and sobbing sound seemed only to bring out more forcibly the utter silence of the tall trees and the sky above them; light wreaths of mist lay over the moat, and we could see far across the rough pasture, with a few scattered oaks of immemorial age standing bluff and gnarled among the grass. The time of fresh spring showers, of sailing clouds, of basking summer heat, was over—so said the grey, gentle sky—what was left but to let the sap run backward to its secret home, to rest, to die? With such sober and stately acquiescence would I await the end, not grudgingly, not impatiently, but in a kind of solemn glory, with gratitude and love and trust.

My companion of that day was Vane, one of my colleagues, and we had discussed a dozen of the small interests and problems that make up our busy life at this restless place; but a silence fell upon us now. The curtain of life was for a moment drawn aside, the hangings that wrap us round, and we looked for an instant into the vast and starlit silences, the formless, ancient dark, where a thousand years are but as yesterday, and into which the countless generations of men have marched, one after another. That is a solemn, but hardly a despairing thought; for something is being wrought out in the silence, something of which we may not be conscious, but which is surely there. Could we but lay that cool and mighty thought closer to our spirits! That impenetrable mystery ought to give us courage, to let us rest, as it were, within a mighty arm. Behind and beyond the precisest creed that great mystery lies; the bewildering question as to how it is possible for our own atomic life to be so sharply defined and bounded from the life of the world—why the frail tabernacle in which we move should be thus intensely our own, and all outside it apart from us.

Yet in days like this calm autumn day one seems to draw a little closer to the mystery, to take a nearer share in the great and wide inheritance, to be less of ourselves and more of God.—Ever yours,

T. B.

MONK'S ORCHARD,
UPTON,
Oct. 12, 1904.

DEAR HERBERT,—I have nothing but local gossip to tell you. We have been having a series of Committee meetings lately about our Chapel services; I am a member of the Committee, and as so often happens when one is brought into close contact with one's colleagues upon a definite question, I find myself lost in bewilderment at the views which are held and advanced by sensible and virtuous men. I don't say that I am necessarily right, and that those who disagree with me are wrong; I daresay that some of my fellow-members think me a tiresome and wrong-headed man. But in one point I believe I am right; in things of this kind, the only policy seems to me to try to arrive at some broad principle, to know what you are driving at; and then, having arrived at it, to try and work it out in detail. Now two or three of my friends seem to me to begin at the wrong end; to have got firmly into their heads certain details, and to fight with all their power to get these details accepted, without attempting to try and develop a principle at all. For instance, Roberts, one of the members of the Committee, is only anxious for what he calls the maintenance of liturgical tradition; he says that there is a science of liturgy, and that it is of the utmost importance to keep in touch with it. The sort of detail that he presses is that at certain seasons the same hymn ought to be sung on Sunday morning and every morning throughout the week, because of the mediaeval system of octaves. He calls this knocking the same nail on the head, and, as is common enough, he is led to confuse a metaphor with an argument. Again, he is very anxious to have the Litany twice a week, that the boys may be trained, as he calls it, in the habit of continuous prayerful attention. Another member, Randall, is very anxious that the services should be what he calls instructive; that courses, for instance, of sermons should be preached on certain books of the Old Testament, on the Pauline Epistles, and so forth. He is also very much set on having dogmatic and doctrinal sermons, because dogma and doctrine are the bone and sinew of religion. Another man, old Pigott, says that the whole theory of worship is praise, and he is very anxious to avoid all subjective and individual religion.

I find myself in hopeless disagreement with these three worthy men; my own theory of school services is, to put it shortly, that they should FEED THE SOUL, and draw it gently to the mysteries of Love and Faith. The whole point is, I believe, to rouse and sustain a pure and generous emotion. Most boys have in various degrees a religious sense. That is to say, that they have moments when they are conscious of the Fatherhood of God, of redemption from sin, of the indwelling of a Holy Spirit. They have moments when they see all that they might be and are not—moments when they would rather be pure than impure, unselfish rather than self-absorbed, kind rather than unkind, brave rather than cowardly; moments when they perceive, however dimly, that happiness lies in activity and kindliness, and when they would give much never to have stained their conscience with evil. It seems to me that school services ought to aim at developing these faint and faltering dreams, at increasing the sense of the beauty and peace of holiness, at giving them some strong and joyful thought that will send them back to the world of life resolved to try again, to be better and worthier.

I am afraid that I do not value the science of liturgical tradition very much. The essence of all science is that it should be progressive; our problems and needs are not the same as mediaeval problems and needs. The whole conception of God and man has broadened and deepened. Science has taught us that nature is a part of the mind of God, not something to be merely contended against; again, it has taught us that man has probably not fallen from grace into corruption, but is slowly struggling upwards out of darkness into light. Again, we no longer think that everything was created for the use and enjoyment of man; we know now of huge tracts of the earth where for thousands of years a vast pageant of life has been displaying itself without any reference to humanity at all. Then, too, as a great scientist has lately pointed out, the dark and haunting sense of sin, that drove devotees to the desert and to lives of the grimmest asceticism, has given place to a nobler conception of civic virtue, has turned men's hearts rather to amendment than to repentance; well, that, in the face of all this, we should be limited to the precise kind of devotions that approved themselves to mediaeval minds seems to me to be a purely retrograde position.

Then as to arranging services in order to cultivate the power of continuous prayer among boys, I think it a thoroughly unpractical theory. In the first place, for one boy so trained you blunt the religious susceptibilities of ninety-nine others. Boys are quick, lively, and bird-like creatures, intolerant above all things of tedium and strain; and I believe that in order to cultivate the religious sense in them, the first duty of all is to make religion attractive, and resolutely to put aside all that tends to make it a weariness.

As to doctrinal and dogmatic instruction, I cannot feel that, at a school, the chapel is the place for that; the boys here get a good deal of religious instruction, and Sunday is already too full, if anything, of it. I believe that the chapel is the place to make them, if possible, love their faith and find it beautiful; and if you can secure that, the dogma will look after itself. The point is, for instance, that a boy should be aware of his redemption, not that he should know the metaphysical method in which it was effected. There is very little dogmatic instruction in the Gospels, and what there is seems to have been delivered to the few and not to the many, to the shepherds rather than to the flocks; it is vital religion and not technical that the chapel should be concerned with.

As to the theory of praise, I cannot help feeling that the old idea that God demanded, so to speak, a certain amount of public recognition of His goodness and greatness is a purely savage and uncivilised form of fetish-worship; it is the same sort of religion that would attach material prosperity to religious observation; and belongs to a time when men believed that, in return for a certain number of sacrifices, rain and sun were sent to the crops of godly persons, with a nicer regard to their development than was applied in the case of the ungodly. The thought of the Father of men feeling a certain satisfaction in their assembling together to roar out in concert somewhat extravagantly phrased ascriptions of honour and majesty seems to me purely childish.

My own belief is that services should in the first place be as short as possible; that there should be variety and interest, plenty of movement and plenty of singing, and that every service should be employed to meet and satisfy the restless minds and bodies of children. But though all should be simple, it should not, I think, be of a plain and obvious type entirely. There are many delicate mysteries, of hope and faith, of affliction and regret, of suffering and sorrow, of which many boys are dimly conscious. There are many subtle and seemly qualities which lie a little apart from the track of manly, full-fed, game-playing boyhood; and such emotions should be cultivated and given voice in our services. To arrange the whole of our religion for brisk, straightforward boys, whose temptations are of an obvious type and who have never known sickness or sorrow is, I believe, a radical mistake. There is a good deal of secret, tender, delicate emotion in the hearts of many boys, which cannot be summarily classed and dismissed as subjective.

Sermons should be brief and ethical, I believe. They should aim at waking generous thoughts and hopes, pure and gracious ideals. Anything of a biographical character appeals strongly to boys; and if one can show that it is not inconsistent with manliness to have a deep and earnest faith, to love truth and purity as well as liberty and honour, a gracious seed has been sown.

Above all, religion should not be treated from the purely boyish point of view; let the boys feel that they are strangers, soldiers, and pilgrims, let them realise that the world is a difficult place, but that there is indeed a golden clue that leads through the darkness of the labyrinth, if they can but set their hand upon it; let them learn to be humble and grateful, not hard and self-sufficient. And, above all, let them realise that things in this world do not come by chance, but that a soul is set in a certain place, and that happiness is to be found by interpreting the events of life rightly, by facing sorrows bravely, by showing kindness, by thankfully accepting joy and pleasure.

And lastly, there should come some sense of unity, the thought of combination for good, of unaffectedness about what we believe to be true and pure, of facing the world together and not toying with it in isolation. All this should be held up to boys.

Even as it is boys grow to love the school chapel, and to think of it in after years as a place where gleams of goodness and power visited them. It might be even more so than it is; but it can only be so, if we realise the conditions, the material with which we are working. We ought to set ourselves to meet and to encourage every beautiful aspiration, every holy and humble thought; not to begin with some eclectic theory, and to try to force boys into the mould. We do that in every other department of school life; but I would have the chapel to be a place of liberty, where tender spirits may be allowed a glimpse of high and holy things which they fitfully desire, and which may indeed prove to be a gate of heaven.

Well, for once I have been able to finish a letter without a single interruption. If my letters, as a rule, seem very inconsequent, remember that they are often written under pressure. But I suppose we each envy the other; you would like a little more pressure and I a little less. I am glad to hear that all goes well; thank Nellie for her letter.—Ever yours,

T. B.

UPTON,
Oct. 19, 1904.

DEAR HERBERT,—I am at present continuously liturgical, owing to my Committee; but you must have the benefit of it.

I have often wondered which of the compilers of the Prayer-book fixed upon the Venite as the first Canticle for our Morning Service; wondered, I say, in the purposeless way that one does wonder, without ever taking the trouble to find out. I dare say there are abundant ecclesiological precedents for it, if one took the trouble to discover them. But the important thing is that it was done; and it is a stroke of genius to have done it. (N.B.—I find it is in the Breviary appointed for Matins.)

The thing is so perfect in itself, and in a way so unexpected, that I feel in the selection of it the work of a deep and poetical heart. Many an ingenious ecclesiastical mind would be afraid of putting a psalm in such a place which changed its mood so completely as the Venite does. To end with a burst of noble and consuming anger, of vehement and merciless indignation—that is the magnificent thing.

Just consider it; I will write down the verses, just for the simple pleasure of shaping the great simple phrases:—

"Oh come let us sing unto the Lord; let us heartily rejoice in the strength of our salvation."

What a vigorous and enlivening verse, like the invitation of old song-writers, "Begone, dull care." For once let us trust ourselves to the full tide of exaltation and triumph, let there be no heavy overshadowings of thought.

"Let us come before his presence with thanksgiving: and show ourselves glad in him with psalms.

"For the Lord is a great God: and a great King above all Gods.

"In his hand are all the corners of the earth; and the strength of the hills is his also.

"The sea is his and he made it; and his hands prepared the dry land.

"Oh come, let us worship, and fall down: and kneel before the Lord our Maker.

"For he is the Lord our God; and we are the people of his pasture and the sheep of his hand."

What a splendid burst of joy; the joy of earth, when the sun is bright in a cloudless heaven, and the fresh wind blows cheerfully across the plain. There is no question of duty here, of a task to be performed in heaviness, but a simple tide of joyfulness such as filled the heart of the poet who wrote:—

"God's in His Heaven;
All's right with the world."

I take it that these verses draw into themselves, as the sea draws the streams, all the rivers of joy and beauty that flow, whether laden with ships out of the heart of great cities, or dropping and leaping from high unvisited moorlands. All the sweet joys that life holds for us find their calm end and haven here; all the delights of life, of action, of tranquil thought, of perception, of love, of beauty, of friendship, of talk, of reflection, are all drawn into one great flood of gratitude and thankfulness; the thankfulness that comes from the thought that after all it is He that made us, and not we ourselves; that we are indeed led and pastured by green meadows and waters of comfort; in such a mood all uneasy anxieties, all dull questionings, die and are merged, and we are glad to be.

Then suddenly falls a different mood, a touch of pathos, in the thought that there are some who from wilfulness, and vain desire, and troubled scheming, shut themselves out from the great inheritance; to them comes the pleading call, the sorrowful invitation:—

"To-day if ye will hear his voice, harden not your hearts; as in the provocation, and as in the day of temptation in the wilderness.

"When your fathers tempted me: proved me, and saw my works."

And then rises the gathering wrath; the doom of all perverse and stubborn natures, who will not yield, or be guided, or led; who live in a wilful sadness, a petty obstinacy:—

"Forty years long was I grieved with this generation, and said: It is a people that do err in their hearts for they have not known my ways."

And then the passion of the mood, the fierce indignation, rises and breaks, as it were, in a dreadful thunderclap:—

"Unto whom I sware in my wrath that they should not enter into my rest."

But even so the very horror of the denunciation holds within it a thought of beauty, like an oasis in a burning desert. "My REST"—that sweet haven which does truly await all those who will but follow and wait upon God.

I declare that the effect of this amazing lyric grows upon me every time that I hear it. Some Psalms, like the delicate and tender cxix., steal into the heart after long and quiet use. How dull I used to find it as a child; how I love it now! But this is not the case with the Venite; its noble simplicity and directness has no touch of intentional subtlety about it. Rather the subtlety was in the true insight, which saw that, if ever there was a Psalm which should at once give the reins to joy, and at the same time pierce the careless heart with a sharp arrow of thought, this was the Psalm.

I feel as if I had been trying in this letter to do as Mr. Interpreter did—to have you into a room full of besoms and spiders, and to draw a pretty moral out of it all. But I am sure that the beauty of this particular Psalm, and of its position, is one of those things that is only spoilt for us by familiarity; and that it is a duty in life to try and break through the crust of familiarity which tends to be deposited round well-known things, and to see how bright and joyful a jewel shows its heart of fire beneath.

I have been hoping for a letter; but no doubt it is all right. I am before my time, I see.—Ever yours,

T. B.

UPTON,
Oct. 25, 1904.

DEAR HERBERT,—I have been studying, with a good deal of interest, two books, the Letters of Professor A——, and the Life of Bishop F——. Given the form, I think the editor of the letters has done his work well. His theory has been to let the Professor speak for himself; while he himself stands, like a discreet and unobtrusive guide, and just says what is necessary in the right place. In this he is greatly to be commended; for it happens too often that biographers of eminent men use their privilege to do a little adventitious self-advertisement. They blow their own trumpets; they stand and posture courteously in the ante-room, when what one desires is to go straight into the presence.

I once had a little piece of biography to do which necessitated my writing requests for reminiscences to several of the friends of the subject of my book. I never had such a strange revelation of human nature. A very few people gave me just what I wanted to know—facts, and sayings, and trenchant actions. A second class of correspondents told me things which had a certain value—episodes in which my hero appeared, but intermingled with many of their own opinions, doings, and sayings. A third class wrote almost exclusively about themselves, using my hero as a peg to hang their own remarks upon. The worst offender of all wrote me long reminiscences of his own conversations, in the following style: "How well I remember the summer of 18—, when dear P—— was staying at F——. I and my wife had a little house in the neighbourhood. We found it convenient to be able to run down there and to rest a little after the fatigues of London life. I remember very well a walk I took with P——. It was the time of the Franco-Prussian War, and I was full of indignation at the terrible sacrifice of life which appeared to me to be for no end. I remember pouring out my thoughts to P——." Here followed a page or two of reflections upon the barbarity of war. "P—— listened to me with great interest; I cannot now recall what he said, but I know that it struck me very much at the time." And so on through many closely written pages.

Well, the editor of the Professor's letters has not done this at all; he keeps himself entirely in the background. But, after reading the book, the reflection is borne in upon me that, unless the hero is a good letter-writer (and the Professor was not), the form of the book cannot be wholly justified. Most of the letters are, so to speak, business letters; they are either letters connected with ecclesiastical politics, or they are letters dealing with technical historical points. There are many little shrewd and humorous turns occurring in them. But these should, I think, have been abstracted from their context and worked into a narrative. The Professor was a man of singular character and individuality. Besides his enormous erudition, he had a great fund of sterling common sense, a deep and liberal piety, and a most inconsequent and, I must add, undignified sense of humour. He carried almost to a vice the peculiarly English trait of national character—the extreme dislike of emotional statement, the inability to speak easily and unaffectedly on matters of strong feeling and tender concern. I confess that this has a displeasing effect. When one desires above all things to have a glimpse into his mind, to be reassured as to his seriousness and piety, it is ten to one that the Professor will, so to speak, pick up his skirts, and execute a series of clumsy, if comic, gambols and caracoles in front of you. A sense of humour is a very valuable thing, especially in a professor of theology; but it should be of a seemly and pungent type, not the humour of a Merry Andrew. And one has the painful sense, especially in the most familiar letters of this collection, that the Professor took an almost puerile pleasure in trying to shock his correspondent, in showing how naughty he could be. One feels the same kind of shock as if one had gone to see the Professor on serious business, and found him riding on a rocking-horse in his study, with a paper cap on his head. There is nothing morally wrong about it; but it appears to be silly, and silliness is out of place behind a gown and under a college cap.

But the Biography of Bishop F—— opens up a further and more interesting question, which I feel myself quite unequal to solving. One has a respect for erudition, of course, but I find myself pondering gloomily over the reasons for this respect. Is it only the respect that one feels for the man who devotes patient labour to the accomplishment of a difficult task, a task which demands great mental power? What I am not clear about is what the precise value of the work of the erudite historian is. The primary value of history is its educational value. It is good for the mind to have a wide view of the world, to have a big perspective of affairs. It corrects narrow, small, personal views; it brings one in contact with heroic, generous persons; it displays noble qualities. It gives one glimpses of splendid self-sacrifice, of lives devoted to a high cause; it sets one aglow with visions of patriotism, liberty and justice. It shows one also the darker side; how great natures can be neutralised or even debased by uncorrected faults; how bigotry can triumph over intelligence; how high hopes can be disappointed. All this is saddening; yet it deepens and widens the mind; it teaches one what to avoid; it brings one near to the deep and patient purposes of God.

But then there is a temptation to think that vivid, picturesque, stimulating writers can do more to develop this side of history than patient, laborious, just writers. One begins to be inclined to forgive anything but dulness in a writer; to value vitality above accuracy, colour above truth. One is tempted to feel that the researches of erudite historians end only in proving that white is not so white, and black not so black as one had thought. That generous persons had a seamy side; that dark and villainous characters had much to be urged in excuse for their misdeeds. This is evidently a wrong frame of mind, and one is disposed to say that one must pursue truth before everything. But then comes in the difficulty that truth is so often not to be ascertained; that documentary evidence is incomplete, and that even documents themselves do not reveal motives. Of course, the perfect combination would be to have great erudition, great common sense and justice, and great enthusiasm and vigour as well. It is obviously a disadvantage to have a historian who suppresses vital facts because they do not fit in with a preconceived view of characters. But still I find it hard to resist the conviction that, from the educational point of view, stimulus is more important than exactness. It is more important that a boy should take a side, should admire and abhor, than that he should have very good reasons for doing so. For it is character and imagination that we want to affect rather than the mastery of minute points and subtleties.

Thus, from an educational point of view, I should consider that Froude was a better writer than Freeman; just as I should consider it more important that a boy should care for Virgil than that he should be sure that he had the best text.

I think that what I feel to be the most desirable thing of all is, that boys should learn somehow to care for history—however prejudiced a view they take of it—when they are young; and that, when they are older, they should correct misapprehensions, and try to arrive at a more complete and just view.

Then I go on to my further point, and here I find myself in a still darker region of doubt. I must look upon it, I suppose, as a direct assault of the Evil One, and hold out the shield of faith against the fiery darts.

What, I ask myself, is, after all, the use of this practice of erudition? What class of the community does it, nay, can it, benefit? The only class that I can even dimly connect with any benefits resulting from it is the class of practical politicians; and yet, in politics, I see a tendency more and more to neglect the philosophical and abstruse view; and to appeal more and more to later precedents, not to search among the origins of things. Nay, I would go further, and say that a pedantic and elaborate knowledge of history hampers rather than benefits the practical politician. It is not so with all the learned professions. The man of science may hope that his researches may have some direct effect in enriching the blood of the world. He may fight the ravages of disease, he may ameliorate life in a hundred ways.

But these exponents of learning, these restorers of ancient texts, these disentanglers of grammatical subtleties, these divers among ancient chronicles and forgotten charters—what is it that they do but to multiply and revive useless knowledge, and to make it increasingly difficult for a man to arrive at a broad and philosophical view, or ever attack his subject at the point where it may conceivably affect humanity or even character? The problem of the modern world is the multiplication of books and records, and every new detail dragged to light simply encumbers the path of the student. I have no doubt that this is a shallow and feeble-minded view. But I am not advancing it as a true view; I am only imploring help; I only desire light. I am only too ready to believe in the virtues and uses of erudition, if any one will point them out to me. But at present it only appears to me like a gigantic mystification, enabling those who hold richly endowed posts to justify themselves to the world, and to keep the patronage of these emoluments in their own hands. Supposing, as a reductio ad absurdum, that some wealthy individual were to endow an institution in order that the members of it might count the number of threads in carpets. One can imagine a philosophical defence being made of the pursuit. A man might say that it was above all things necessary to classify, and investigate, and to arrive at the exact truth; to compare the number of threads in different carpets, and that the sordid difficulties which encumbered such a task should not be regarded, in the light of the fact that here, at least, exact results had been obtained.

Of course, that is all very silly! But I believe; only I want my unbelief helped! If you can tell me what services are rendered by erudition to national life, you will relieve my doubts. Do not merely say that it enlarges the bounds of knowledge, unless you are also prepared to prove that knowledge is, per se, a desirable thing. I am not sure that it is not a hideous idol, a Mumbo Jumbo, a Moloch in whose honour children have still to pass through the fire in the recesses of dark academic groves.—Ever yours,

T. B.

UPTON,
Nov. 1, 1904.

MY DEAR HERBERT,—I have read, after a fashion, in the course of the last month, the Autobiography of Herbert Spencer. I know nothing of his philosophy—I doubt if I have read half-a-dozen pages of his writings; and the man, as revealed in his own transparent confessions, is almost wholly destitute of attractiveness. All the same it is an intensely interesting book, because it is the attempt of a profound egotist to give a perfectly sincere picture of his life. Of course, I should have read it with greater appreciation if I had studied or cared for his books; but I take for granted that he was a great man, and accomplished a great work, and I like to see how he achieved it.

The book is the strongest argument I have ever yet read against a rational education. I who despair of the public-school classical system, am reluctantly forced to confess that it can sow the seeds of fairer flowers than ever blossomed in the soul of Herbert Spencer. He was by no means devoid of aesthetic perception. He says that the sight of a mountain, and music heard in a cathedral were two of the things that moved him most. He describes a particular sunset which he saw in Scotland, and describes the experience as the climax of his emotional sensations. He was devoted to music, and had a somewhat contemptuous enjoyment of pictures. But the arrogance and impenetrability of the man rise up on every page. He cannot say frankly that he does not understand art and literature; he dogmatises about them, and gives the reader to understand that there is really nothing in them. He criticises the classics from the standpoint of a fourth form boy. He sits like a dry old spider, spinning his philosophical web, with a dozen avenues of the soul closed to him, and denying that such avenues exist. As a statistical and sociological expert he ought to have taken into account the large number of people who are affected by what we may call the beautiful, and to have allowed for its existence even if he could not feel it. But no, he is perfectly self-satisfied, perfectly decided. And this is the more surprising because the man was in reality a hedonist. He protests finely in more than one place against those who make life subsidiary to work. He is quite clear on the point that work is only a part of life, and that to live is the object of man. Again, he states that the pursuit of innocent pleasure is a thing to which it is justifiable to devote some energy, and yet this does not make him tolerant. The truth is that he was so supremely egotistical, so entirely wrapped up in himself and his own life, that what other people did and cared for was a matter of entire indifference to him. His social tastes, and they were considerable, were all devoted to one and the same purpose. He liked staying at agreeable country houses, because it was a pleasant distraction to him and improved his health. He liked dining out, because it stimulated his digestion. All human relationships are made subservient to the same end. It never seems to him to be a duty to minister to the pleasure of others. He takes what he can get at the banquet of life, and, having secured his share, goes away to digest it. When, at the end of his life, social entertainments tried his nerves, he gave them up. When people came to see him, and he found himself getting tired or excited by conversation, if it was not convenient to him to leave the room, he put stoppers in his ears to blur the sense of the talk. What better parable of the elaborate framework of egotism on which his life was constructed could there be than the following legend, not derived from the book? One evening, the story goes, the philosopher had invited, at his club, a youthful stranger to join him in a game of billiards. The young man, who was a proficient, ran out in two breaks, leaving his rival a hopeless distance behind. When he had finished, Spencer, with a severe air, said to him: "To play billiards in an ordinary manner is an agreeable adjunct to life; to play as you have been playing is evidence of a misspent youth." A man who was not an egotist and a philosopher, however much he disliked the outcome of the game, would have attempted some phrases of commendation. But Spencer's view was, that anything which rendered a player of billiards less useful to himself, by giving him fewer opportunities in the course of a game for what he would have called healthful and pleasurable recreation, was not only not to be tolerated, but was to be morally reprobated.

As to his health, a subject which occupies the larger part of the volumes, it is evident that, though his nervous system was deranged, he was a complete hypochondriac. There is very little repining about the invalid conditions under which he lived; and it gradually dawned upon me that this was not because he had resolved to bear it in a stoical and courageous manner, but because his ill-health, seen through the rosy spectacles of the egotist, was a matter of pleasurable excitement to him; he complains a good deal of the peculiar sensations he experienced, and his broken nights, but with a solemn satisfaction in the whole experience. He never had to bear physical pain, and the worst evil from which he suffered was the boredom resulting from the way in which he had to try, or conceived that he had to try, to kill time without reading or working.

Of course one cannot help admiring the tenacious way in which he carried out his great work under unfavourable conditions. Yet there is something ridiculous in the picture of his rowing about in a boat on the Regent's Park Lake, with an amanuensis in the stern, dictating under the lee of an island until his sensations returned, and then rowing until they subsided again. As a hedonist, he distinctly calculated that his work gave the spice to his life, and that he would not have been so happy had he relinquished it. But there is nothing generous or noble about his standpoint; he liked writing and philosophising, and he preferred to do it even though it entailed a certain amount of invalidism, in the same spirit in which a man prefers to drink champagne with the prospect of suffering from the gout, rather than to renounce champagne and gout alike.

The man's face is in itself a parable. He has the high, domed forehead of the philosopher, and a certain geniality of eye; but the hard, thin-lipped mouth, with the deep lines from the nose, give him the air of an elderly chimpanzee. He has a hand like a bird's claw; and the antique shirt-front and small bow-tie denote the man who has fixed his opinions on the cut of his clothes at an early date and does not intend to modify them. Quite apart from the intense seriousness with which the sage took himself, down to the smallest details, the style of the book, dry as it is, is in itself grotesquely attractive.

There is something in the use of solemn scientific terminology, when dealing with the most trivial matters, which makes many passages irresistibly ludicrous. I wish that I could think that the writer of the following lines wrote them with any consciousness of how humorous a passage he was constructing—

"With me any tendency towards facetiousness is the result of temporary elation, either ... caused by pleasurable health-giving change, or more commonly by meeting old friends. Habitually I observed that on seeing the Lotts after a long interval, I was apt to give vent to some witticisms during the first hour or two, and then they became rare."

I can't say that the life is a sad one, because, on the whole, it is a contented one; but it is so one-sided and so self-absorbed that one feels dried-up and depressed by it. One feels that great ability, great perseverance, may yet leave a man very cold and hard; that a man may penetrate the secrets of philosophy and yet never become wise; and one ends by feeling that simplicity, tenderness, a love of beautiful and gracious things are worth far more than great mental achievement. Or rather, I suppose, that one has to pay a price for everything, and that the price that this dyspeptic philosopher paid for his great work was to move through the world in a kind of frigid blindness, missing life after all, and bartering reality for self-satisfaction.

Curiously enough, I have at the same time been reading the life of another self-absorbed and high-minded personality—the late Dean Farrar. This is a book the piety of which is more admirable than the literary skill; but probably the tender partiality with which it is written makes it a more valuable document from the point of view of revealing personality than if it had been more critically treated.

Farrar was probably the exact opposite of Herbert Spencer in almost every respect. He was a litterateur, a rhetorician, an idealist, where Spencer was a philosopher, a scientific man, and a rationalist. Farrar admired high literature with all his heart; though unfortunately it did not clarify his own taste, but only gave him a rich vocabulary of high-sounding words, which he bound into a flaunting bouquet. He was like the bower-bird, which takes delight in collecting bright objects of any kind, bits of broken china, fragments of metal, which it disposes with distressing prominence about its domicile, and runs to and fro admiring the fantastic pattern. The fabric of Farrar's writing is essentially thin; his thoughts rarely rose above the commonplace, and to these thoughts he gave luscious expression, sticking the flowers of rhetoric, of which his marvellous memory gave him the command, so as to ornament without adorning.

Every one must have been struck in Farrar's works of fiction by the affected tone of speech adopted by his saintly and high-minded heroes. It was not affectation in Farrar to speak and write in this way; it was the form in which his thoughts naturally arranged themselves. But in one sense it was affected, because Farrar seems to have been naturally a kind of dramatist. I imagine that his self-consciousness was great, and I expect that he habitually lived with the feeling of being the central figure in a kind of romantic scene. The pathos of the situation is that he was naturally a noble-minded man. He had a high conception of beauty, both artistic and moral beauty. He did live in the regions to which he directed others. But this is vitiated by a desire for recognition, a definite, almost a confessed, ambition. The letter, for instance, in which he announces that he has accepted a Canonry at Westminster is a painful one. If he felt the inexpressible distress, of which he speaks, at the idea of leaving Marlborough, there was really no reason why he should not have stayed; and, later on, his failure to attain to high ecclesiastical office seems to have resulted in a sense of compassion for the inadequacy of those who failed to discern real merit, and a certain bitterness of spirit which, considering his services to religion and morality, was not wholly unnatural. But he does not seem to have tried to interpret the disappointment that he felt, or to have asked himself whether the reason of his failure did not rather lie in his own temperament.

The kindness of the man, his laboriousness, his fierce indignation against moral evil, to say nothing of his extraordinary mental powers, seem to have been clogged all through life by this sad self-consciousness. The pity and the mystery of it is that a man should have been so moulded to help his generation, and then that this grievous defect of temperament should have been allowed to take its place as the tyrant of the whole nature. And what makes the whole situation even more tragic is that it was through a certain transparency of nature that this egotism became apparent to others. He was a man who seemed bound to speak of all that was in his mind; that was a part of his rhetorical temperament. But if he could have held his tongue, if he could have kept his own weakness of spirit concealed, he might have achieved the very successes which he desired, and, indeed, deserved. The result is that a richly endowed character achieves no conspicuous greatness, either as a teacher, a speaker, a writer, or even as a man.

The moral of these two books is this: How can any one whose character is deeply tinged by this sort of egotism—and it is the shadow of all eager and sensitive temperaments—best fight against it? Can it be subdued, can it be concealed, can it be cured? I hardly dare to think so. But I think that a man may deliberately resolve not to make recognition an object; and next I believe he may most successfully fight against egotism in ordinary life by regarding it mainly as a question of manners. If a man can only, in early life, get into his head that it is essentially bad manners to thrust himself forward, and determine rather to encourage others to speak out what is in their minds, a habit can be acquired; and probably, upon acquaintance, an interest in the point of view of others will grow. That is not a very lofty solution, but I believe it to be a practical one; and certainly for a man of egotistic nature it is a severe and fruitful lesson to read the lives of two such self-absorbed characters as Spencer and Farrar, and to see, in the one case, how ugly and distorting a fault, in the other, how hampering a burden it may become.

Egotism is really a failure of sympathy, a failure of justice, a failure of proportion, and to recognise this is the first step towards establishing a desire to be loving, just, and well-balanced.

But still the mystery remains: and I think that perhaps the most wholesome attitude is to be grateful for what in the way of work, of precept, of example these men achieved, and to leave the mystery of their faults to their Maker, in the noble spirit of Gray's Elegy:—

"No farther seek his merits to disclose,
    Or draw his frailties from their dread abode
(There they alike in trembling hope repose),
    The bosom of his Father and his God."

—Ever yours,

T. B.

MONK'S ORCHARD,
UPTON,
Nov. 8, 1904.

DEAR HERBERT,—I have been trying to read the letters of T. E. Brown. Do you know anything about him? He was a Manxman by birth, a fellow of Oriel, a Clifton Master for many years, and at the end of his life a Manxman again—he held a living there. He wrote some spirited tales in verse, in the Manx vernacular, and he was certainly a poet at heart. He was fond of music, and a true lover of nature. He had a genius for friendship, and evidently had the gift of inspiring other people; high-minded and intelligent men speak of him, in the little memoir that precedes the letters, with a pathetic reverence and a profound belief in the man's originality, and even genius. I was so sure that I should enjoy the book that I ordered it before it was published, and, when it appeared, it was a very profound disappointment. I don't mean to say that there are not beautiful things in it; it shows one a wholesome nature and a grateful, kindly heart; but, in the first place, he writes a terrible style, the kind of style that imposes on simple people because it is allusive, and what is called unconventional; to me it is simply spasmodic and affected. The man seems, as a rule, utterly unable to say anything in a simple and delicate way; his one object appears to be not to use the obvious word. He has a sort of jargon of his own—a dreadful jargon. He must write "crittur" or "craythur," when he means "creature"; he says "Yiss, ma'am, I'd be glad to jine the Book Club"; he uses the word "galore"; he talks of "the resipiscential process" when he means growing wiser—at least I think that is what he means. The following, taken quite at random, are specimens of the sort of passages that abound:—

"Rain, too, is one of my joys. I want to wash myself, soak myself in it; hang myself over a meridian to dry; dissolve (still better) into rags of soppy disintegration, blotting paper, mash and splash and hash of inarticulate protoplasm."

I suppose that both he and his friends thought that picturesque; to me it is neither beautiful nor amusing—simply ugly and aggravating.

Here again:—

"On the Quantocks I feel fairies all round me, the good folk, meet companions for young poets. How Coleridge, more especially, fits in to such surroundings! 'Fairies?' say you. Well, there's odds of fairies, and of the sort I mean Coleridge was the absolute Puck. 'Puck?' says you. 'For shame!' says you. No, d—n it! I'll stick to that. There's odds o' fairies, and often enough I think the world is nothing else; troops, societies, hierarchies—S.T.C., a supreme hierarch; look at his face; think of meeting him at moonlight between Stowey and Alfoxden, like a great white owl, soft and plumy, with eyes of flame!"

I confess that such passages simply make me blush, leave me with a kind of mental nausea. What makes it worse is that there is something in what he says, if he would only say it better. It makes me feel as I should feel if I saw an elderly, heavily-built clergyman amusing himself in a public place with a skipping-rope, to show what a child of nature he was.

I cannot help feeling that the man was a poseur, and that his affectations were the result of living in a small and admiring coterie. If, when one begins to write and talk in that jesting way, there is some one at your elbow to say, "How refreshing, how original, how rugged!" I suppose that one begins to think that one had better indulge oneself in such absurdities. But readers outside the circle turn away in disgust.

The pity of it is that Brown had something of the Celtic spirit—the melancholy, the mystery of that sensitive and delicate temperament; but it is vitiated by what I can only call a schoolmaster's humour—cheap and silly, such as imposes on immature minds. When he was quite serious and simple, he wrote beautiful, quiet, wise letters, dealing with deep things in a dignified way; but, as a rule, he thought it necessary to cut ugly capers, and to do what can only be described as playing the fool. I wish with all my heart that these letters had not been published; they deform and disfigure a beautiful spirit and a quick imagination.

Pose, affectation—what a snare they are to the better kind of minds. I declare that I value every day more and more the signs of simplicity, the people who say what they mean, and as they mean it; who don't think what they think is expected of them, but what they really feel; who don't pretend to enjoy what they don't enjoy, or to understand what they don't understand.

I may be all wrong about Brown, of course, for the victory always remains with the people who admire, rather than with the people who criticise; people cannot be all on the same plane, and it is of no use to quench enthusiasm by saying, "When you are older and wiser you will think differently." The result of that kind of snub is only to make people hold their tongues, and think one an old-fashioned pedant. I sometimes wonder whether there is an absolute standard of beauty at all, whether taste is not a sort of epidemic contagion, and whether the accredited man of taste is not, as some one says, the man who has the good fortune to agree most emphatically with the opinion of the majority.

I am sure, however, you would not like the book; though I don't say that you might not extract, as I do to my shame, a kind of bitter pleasure in thinking how unconsciously absurd it is—the pleasure one gets from watching the movements and gestures, and listening to the remarks of a profoundly affected and complacent person. But that is not an elevated kind of pleasure, when all is said and done!

> "We get no good,
> By being ungenerous, even to a book!"

as Mrs. Browning says....—Ever yours.

T. B.

UPTON,
Nov. 15, 1904.

MY DEAR HERBERT,—A controversy, a contest! How they poison all one's thoughts! I am at present wading, as Ruskin says, in a sad marsh or pool of thought. Let me indicate to you without excessive detail the kind of thing that is going on.

We have been discussing the introduction here of certain important educational reforms, in the direction of modernising and simplifying our curriculum.

Now we are all one body here, no doubt, like the Christian Church in the hymn; but unhappily, and unlike the hymn, we ARE very much divided. We are in two camps. There is a conservative section who, doubtless for very good reasons, want to keep things as they are; they see strongly all the blessings of the old order; they like the old ways and believe in them; they think, for instance, that the old classical lines of education are the best, that the system fortifies the mind, and that, when you have been through it, you have got a good instrument which enables you to tackle anything else; a very coherent position, and, in the case of our conservatives, very conscientiously administered.

Then there is a strong Progressive party numerically rather stronger, to which I myself belong. We believe that things might be a good deal better. We are dissatisfied with our results. We think, to take the same instance, that classics are a very hard subject, and that a great many boys are not adapted to profit by them; we believe that the consequence of boys being kept at a hard subject, which they cannot penetrate or master, leads to a certain cynicism about intellectual things, and that the results of a classical education on many boys are so negative that at all events some experiments ought to be tried.

Well, if all discussions could be conducted patiently, good-humouredly, and philosophically, no harm would be done; but they can't! Men will lose their temper, indulge in personalities, and import bitterness into the question. Moreover, a number of my fiercest opponents are among my best friends here, and that is naturally very painful. Indeed, I feel how entirely unfitted I am for these kinds of controversy. This disgusting business deprives me of sleep, makes me unable to concentrate my mind upon my work, destroys both my tranquillity and my philosophy.

It is a relief to write to you on the subject. Yet I don't see my way out. One must have an opinion about one's life-work. My business is education, and I have tried to use my eyes and see things as they are. I am quite prepared to admit that I may be wrong; but if everybody who formed opinions abstained from expressing them out of deference to the people who were not prepared to admit that they themselves could be mistaken, there would be an end of all progress. Minds of the sturdy, unconvinced order are generally found to range themselves on the side of things as they are; and that is at all events a good guarantee that things won't move too fast, and against the trying of rash experiments.

But I don't want to be rash; I think that for a great many boys our type of education is a failure, and I want to see if something cannot be devised to meet their needs. But my opponents won't admit any failure. They say that the boys who, I think, end by being hopelessly uneducated would be worse off if they had not been grounded in the classics. They say that my theory is only to make things easier for boys; and they add that, if any boy's education is an entire failure (they admit a few incapables are to be found), it is the boy's own fault; he has been idle and listless; if he had worked properly it would have been all right; he would have been fortified; and anyhow, they say, it doesn't matter what you teach such boys—they would have been hopeless anyhow.

Of course the difficulty of proving my case is great. You can't, in education, get two exactly parallel boys and try the effect of different types of education on the two. A chemist can put exactly the same quantity of some salt in two vessels, and, by treating them in different ways, produce a demonstration which is irrefragable. But no two boys are exactly alike, and, while classics are demanded at the university, boys of ability will tend to keep on the classical side; so that the admitted failure of modern sides in many places to produce boys of high intellectual ability results from the fact that boys of ability do not tend to join the modern sides.

So one hammers on, and, as it is always easier to leave an object at rest than to set it moving, we remain very much where we were.

The cynical solution is to say, let us have peace at any cost; let the thing alone; let us teach what we have to teach, and not bother about results. But that appears to me to be a cowardly attitude. If one expresses dissatisfaction to one of the cheerful stationary party, they reply, "Oh, take our word for it, it is all right; do your best; you don't teach at all badly, though you lack conviction; leave it to us, and never mind the discontent expressed by parents, and the cynical contempt felt by boys for intellectual things."

"Meanwhile, regardless of their doom,
    The little victims play."

They do indeed! they find work so dispiriting a business that they put it out of their thoughts as much as they can. And when they grow up, conscious of intellectual feebleness, they have no idea of expressing their resentment at the way they have been used—if they are modest, they think that it is their own fault; if they are complacent, they think that intellectual things don't matter.

While I write there comes in one of my cheerful opponents to discuss the situation. We plunge into the subject of classics. I say that, to boys without aptitude, they are dreary and hopelessly difficult. "There you go again," he says, "always wanting to make things EASIER: the thing to do is to keep boys at hard, solid work; it is an advantage that they can't understand what they are working at; it is a better gymnastic." The subject of mathematics is mentioned, and my friend incidentally confesses that he never had the least idea what higher Algebra was all about.

I refrain from saying what comes into my mind. Supposing that he, without any taste for Mathematics, had been kept year after year at them, surely that would have been acting on his principle, viz. to find out what boys can't do and make them do it. No doubt he would say that his mind had been fortified, as it was, by classics. But, if a rigid mathematical training had been employed, his mind might have been fortified into an enviable condition of inaccessibility. But I don't say this; he would only think I was making fun of the whole thing.

Fun, indeed! There is very little amusement to be derived from the situation. My opponents have a strong sense of what they call liberty— which means that every one should have a vote, and that every one should register it in their favour. Or they are like the old-fashioned Whigs, who had a strong belief in popular liberty, and an equally unshaken belief in their own personal superiority.—Ever yours,

T. B.

UPTON,
Nov. 22, 1904.

DEAR HERBERT,—"Be partner of my dreams as of my fishing," says the old fisherman to his mate, in that delicious idyll of Theocritus—do read it again. It is one of the little masterpieces that hang for ever in one of the inner secret rooms of the great halls of poetry. The two old men lie awake in their wattled cabin, listening to the soft beating of the sea, and beguiling the dark hour before the dawn, when they must fare forth, in simple talk about their dreams. It is a genre picture, full of simple detail, but with a vein of high poetry about it; all remote from history and civic life, in that eternal region of perfect and quiet art, into which, thank God, one can always turn to rest awhile.

But to-day I don't want to talk of fishermen, or Theocritus, or even art; I want you to share one of my dreams.

I must preface it by saying that I have just experienced a severe humiliation; I have been deeply wounded. I won't trouble you with the sordid details, but it has been one of those severe checks one sometimes experiences, when a mirror is held up to one's character, and one sees an ugly sight. Never mind that now! But you can imagine my frame of mind.

I bicycled off alone in the afternoon, feeling very sore and miserable in spirit. It was one of those cool, fresh, dark November days, not so much gloomy as half-lit and colourless. There was not a breath stirring. The long fields, the fallows, with hedges and coverts, melted into a light mist, which hid all the distant view. I moved in a narrow twilight circle, myself the centre; the road was familiar enough to me; at a certain point there is a little lodge, with a road turning off to a farm. It is many years since I visited the place, but I remembered dimly that there was some interest of antiquity about the house, and I determined to explore it. The road curved away among quiet fields, with here and there a belt of woodland, then entered a little park; there I saw a cluster of buildings on the edge of a pool, all grown up with little elms and ashes, now bare of leaves. Here I found a friendly, gaitered farmer, who, in reply to my question whether I could see the place, gave me a cordial invitation to come in; he took me to a garden door, opened it, and beckoned me to go through. I found myself in a place of incomparable beauty. It was a long terrace, rather wild and neglected; below there were the traces of a great, derelict garden, with thick clumps of box, the whole surrounded by a large earthwork, covered with elms. To the left lay another pool; to the right, at the end of the terrace, stood a small red-brick chapel, with a big Perpendicular window. The house was to the left of us, in the centre of the terrace, of old red brick, with tall chimneys and mullioned windows. My friend the farmer chatted pleasantly about the house, but was evidently prouder of his rose-trees and his chrysanthemums. The day grew darker as we wandered, and a pleasant plodding and clinking of horses coming home made itself heard in the yard. Then he asked me to enter the house. What was my surprise when he led me into a large hall, with painted panels and a painted ceiling, occupying all the centre of the house. He told me a little of the history of the place, of a visit paid by Charles the First, and other simple traditions, showing me all the time a quiet, serious kindness, which reminded one of the entertainment given to the wayfarers of the Pilgrim's Progress.

Once more we went out on the little terrace and looked round; the night began to fall, and lights began to twinkle in the house, while the fire glowed and darted in the hall.

But what I cannot, I am afraid, impart to you is the strange tranquillity that came softly down into my mind; everything took its part in this atmosphere of peace. The overgrown terrace, the mellow brickwork, the bare trees, the tall house, the gentle kindliness of my host. And then I seemed so far away from the world; there was nothing in sight but the fallows and the woods, rounded with mist; it seemed at once the only place in the world, and yet out of it. The old house stood patiently waiting, serving its quiet ends, growing in beauty every year, seemingly so unconscious of its grace and charm, and yet, as it were, glad to be loved. It seemed to give me just the calm, the tenderness I wanted. To assure me that, whatever pain and humiliation there were in the world, there was a strong and loving Heart behind. My host said good-bye to me very kindly, begging me to come again and bring any one to see the place. "We are very lonely here, and it does us good to see a stranger."

I rode away, and stopped at a corner where a last view of the house was possible; it stood regarding me, it seemed, mournfully, and yet with a solemn welcome from its dark windows. And here was another beautiful vignette; close to me, by a hedge, stood an old labourer, a fork in one hand, the other shading his eyes, watching with simple intentness a flight of wild-duck that was passing overhead, dipping to some sequestered pool.

I rode away with a quiet hopefulness in my heart. I seemed like a dusty and weary wayfarer, who has flung off his heated garments and plunged into the clear waters of comfort; to have drawn near to the heart of the world; to have had a sight, in the midst of things mutable and disquieting, of things august and everlasting. At another time I might have flung myself into busy fancies, imagined a community living an orderly and peaceful life, full of serene activities, in that still place; but for once I was content to have seen a dwelling-place, devised by some busy human brain, that had failed of its purpose, lost its ancient lords, sunk into a calm decay; to have seen it all caressed and comforted and embraced by nature, its scars hidden, its grace replenished, its harshness smoothed away.

Such gentle hours are few; and fewer still the moments of anxiety and vexation when so direct a message is flashed straight from the Mind of God into the unquiet human heart; I never doubted that I was led there by a subtle, delicate, and fatherly tenderness, and shown a thing which should at once touch my sense of beauty, and then rising, as it were, and putting the superficial aspect aside, speak with no uncertain voice of the deep hopes, the everlasting peace on which for a few years the little restless world of ours is rocked and carried to and fro....—Ever yours,

T. B.

UPTON,
Nov. 29, 1904.

DEAR HERBERT,—To-day the world is shrouded in a thick, white, dripping mist. Glancing up in the warm room where I sit, I see nothing but grey window spaces. "How melancholy, how depressing," says my generally cheerful friend, Randall, staring sadly out into the blank air. But I myself do not agree. I am conscious of a vague, pleasurable excitement; a sense, too, of repose. This half light is grateful and cooling alike to eye and brain. Then, too, it is a change from ordinary conditions, and a change has always something invigorating about it. I steal about with an obscure sense that something mysterious is happening. And yet imagine some bright spirit of air and sunshine, like Ariel, flitting hither and thither above the mist, dipping his feet in the vapour, as a sea-bird flies low across the sea. Think of the pity he would feel for the poor human creatures, buried in darkness below, creeping hither and thither in the gloom.

It is pleasurable enough within the house, but still more pleasurable to walk abroad; the little circle of dim vision passes with you, just revealing the road, the field, the pasture in which you walk.

There is a delightful surprise about the way in which a familiar object looms up suddenly, a dim remote shape, and then as swiftly reveals the well-known outline. My path takes me past the line, and I hear a train that I cannot see roar past. I hear the sharp crack of the fog signals and the whistle blown. I pass close to the huge, dripping signals; there, in a hut beside a brazier, sits a plate-layer with his pole, watching the line, ready to push the little disc off the metals if the creaking signal overhead moves. In another lonely place stands a great luggage train waiting. The little chimney of the van smokes, and I hear the voices of guards and shunters talking cheerily together. I draw nearer home, and enter the college by the garden entrance. The black foliage of the ilex lowers overhead, and then in a moment, out of an overshadowing darkness, rises a battlemented tower like a fairy castle, with lights in the windows streaming out with straight golden rays into the fog. Below, the arched doorway reveals the faintly-lighted arches of the cloisters. The hanging, clinging, soaking mist—how it heightens the value, the comfort of the lighted windows of studious, fire-warmed rooms.

And then what a wealth of pleasant images rises in the mind. I find myself thinking how the reading of certain authors is like this mist-walking; one seems to move in a dreary, narrow circle, and then suddenly a dim horror of blackness stands up; and then, again, in a moment one sees that it is some familiar thought which has thus won a stateliness, a remote mystery, from the atmosphere out of which it leans.

Or, better still, how like these fog-wrapped days are to seasons of mental heaviness, when the bright, distant landscape is all swallowed up and cherished landmarks disappear. One walks in a vain shadow; and then the surprises come; something, which in its familiar aspect stirs no tangible emotion, in an instant overhangs the path, shrouded in dim grandeur and solemn awe. Days of depression have this value, that they are apt to reveal the sublimity, the largeness of well-known thoughts, all veiled in a melancholy magnificence. Then, too, one gains an inkling of the sweetness of the warm corners, the lighted rooms of life, the little centre of brightness which one can make in one's own retired heart, and which gives the sense of welcome, the quiet delights of home-keeping, the warmth of the contented mind.

And, best of all, as one stumbles along the half-hidden street a shape, huge, intangible, comes stealing past; one wonders what strange visitant this is that comes near in the gathering darkness. And then in a moment the vagueness is dispelled; the form, the lineaments, take shape from the gloom, and one finds that one is face to face with a familiar friend, whose greeting warms the heart as one passes into the mist again.—Ever yours,

T. B.

UPTON,
Dec. 5, 1904.

MY DEAR HERBERT,—I am very sorry to hear you have been suffering
from depression; it is one of the worst evils of life, and none the better for
being so intangible. I was reading a story the other day, in some old book,
of a moody man who was walking with a friend, and, after a long silence,
suddenly cried out, as if in pain. "What ails you?" said his friend. "My
mind hurts me," said the other. That is the best way to look at it, I think—
as a kind of neuralgia of the soul, to be treated like other neuralgias. A
friend of mine who was a great sufferer from such depression went to an
old doctor, who heard his story with a smile, and then said: "Now, you're
not as bad as you feel, or even as you think. My prescription is a simple
one. Don't eat pastry; and for a fortnight don't do anything you don't like."

It is often only a kind of cramp, and needs an easier position. Try and get a
little change; read novels; don't get tired; sit in the open air. "A recumbent
position," said a witty lady of my acquaintance, "is a great aid to
cheerfulness."

I used, as you know, to be a great sufferer; or perhaps you don't know, for
I was too miserable sometimes even to speak of it. But I can say humbly
and gratefully that a certain freedom from depression is one of the
blessings that advancing years have brought me. Still, I don't altogether
escape, and it sometimes falls with an unexpected suddenness. It may help
you to know that other people suffer similarly, and how they suffer.

Well, then, a few days ago I woke early, after troubled dreams, and knew
that the old enemy had clutched me. I lay in a strange agony of mind, my
heart beating thick, and with an insupportable weight on my heart. It
always takes the same form with me—an overwhelming sense of failure in
all that I attempt, a dreary consciousness of absolute futility, coupled with
the sense of the brevity and misery of human life generally. I ask myself
what is the use of anything? What is an almost demoniacal feature of the
mood is that it lays a spell of utter dreariness upon all pleasures as well as
duties. One feels condemned to a long perspective of work without
interest, and recreation without relish, and all confined and bounded by
death; whichever way my thoughts turned, a grey prospect met me.

Little by little the misery abated, recurring at longer and longer intervals,
till at last I slept again; but the mood overclouded me all day long, and I

went about my duties with indifference. But there is one medicine which hardly ever fails me—it was a half-holiday, and, after tea, I went to the cathedral and sate in a remote corner of the nave. The service had just begun. The nave was dimly lighted, but an upward radiance gushed behind the screen and the tall organ, and lit up the vaulted roof with a tranquil glory. Soon the Psalms began, and at the sound of the clear voices of the choir, which seemed to swim on the melodious thunder of the organ, my spirit leapt into peace, as a man drowning in a stormy sea is drawn into a boat that comes to rescue him. It was the fourth evening, and that wonderful Psalm, My God, my God, look upon me—where the broken spirit dives to the very depths of darkness and despair—brought me the message of triumphant sorrow. How strange that these sad cries of the heart, echoing out of the ages, set to rich music—it was that solemn A minor chant by Battishill, which you know—should be able to calm and uplift the grieving spirit. The thought rises into a burst of gladness at the end; and then follows hard upon it the tenderest of all Psalms, The Lord is my Shepherd, in which the spirit casts its care upon God, and walks simply, in utter trust and confidence. The dreariness of my heart thawed and melted into peace and calm. Then came the solemn murmur of a lesson; the Magnificat, sung to a setting—again as by a thoughtful tenderness—of which I know and love every note; and here my heart seemed to climb into a quiet hope and rest there; the lesson again, like the voice of a spirit; and then the Nunc Dimittis, which spoke of the beautiful rest that remaineth. Then the quiet monotone of prayer, and then, as though to complete my happiness, Mendelssohn's Hear my prayer. It is the fashion, I believe, for some musicians to speak contemptuously of this anthem, to say that it is over-luscious. I only know that it brings all Heaven about me, and reconciles the sadness of the world with the peace of God. A boy's perfect treble—that sweetest of all created sounds, because so unconscious of its pathos and beauty—floating on the top of the music, and singing as an angel might sing among the stars of heaven, came to my thirsty spirit like a draught of clear spring water. And, at the end of all, Mendelssohn's great G major fugue gave the note of courage and endurance that I needed, the strong notes marching solemnly and joyfully on their appointed way.

I left the cathedral, through the gathering twilight, peaceful, hopeful, and invigorated, as a cripple dipped in the healing well. While music is in the world, God abides among us. Ever since the day that David soothed Saul by his sweet harp and artless song, music has thus beguiled the heaviness of the spirit. Yet there is the mystery, that the emotion seems to soar so much higher and dive so much deeper than the notes that evoke it! The best argument for immortality, I think.

Now that I have written so much, I feel that I am, perhaps, inconsiderate in speaking so much of the healing music which you cannot obtain. But get your wife to play to you, in a quiet and darkened room, some of the things you love best. It is not the same as the cathedral, with all its glory and its ancient, dim tradition, but it will serve.

And, meanwhile, think as little of your depression as you can; it won't poison the future; just endure it like a present pain; the moment one can do that, the victory is almost won.

The worst of the grim mood is that it seems to tear away all the pretences with which we beguile our sadness, and to reveal the truth. But it is only that truth which lies at the bottom of the well; and there are fathoms of clear water lying above it, which are quite as true as the naked fact below. That is all the philosophy I can extract from such depression, and, in some mysterious way, it helps us, after all, when it is over; makes us stronger, more patient, more compassionate; and it is worth some suffering, if one lays hold of true experience instead of wasting time in querulous self-commiseration.—Affectionately yours,

T. B.

UPTON,
Dec. 12, 1904.

MY DEAR HERBERT,—I have lately been reading in a whimsical and discursive fashion—you know the mood—turning the pages, and yet not finding the repose one demands in a book.

One thought emerges from such hours; and as I cannot to-day write you a long letter, I will just try and shape my ideas in a few sentences, hoping that you will be able to supplement or correct it.

Is not the one thing which, after all, one demands in art, PERSONALITY? A perfectly sincere and direct point of view? It matters little what the point of view is, and whether one agrees with it or not, so long as one is certain of its truth and reality. Books where there is any sense of pose, of affectation, of insincerity, do not ever really please or satisfy; of course there are books which are entirely sincere which are yet so unsympathetic that one cannot get near them. But presupposing a certain sympathy of aim and ideal, one may disagree with, or think incomplete, or consider overstrained, the sincere presentment of some thought, but one realises it to be true and natural—to be THERE.

Well, such a point of view holds both hope and discouragement for a writer. Writers have long periods, I suppose, when they don't seem to have anything to say; or, even worse, when they have something to say but can't please themselves as to the manner of saying it. But all these delays, these inarticulate silences, these dumb discouragements are part, after all, of the same thing. It is useless to try and say anything under these conditions; or, if one does contrive to express something, one must look upon it merely as an exercise in expression, a piece of training, a sort of gymnastic—and be content to throw the thing aside.

The only kind of thing that is worth saying is the thing that is conceived in perfect sincerity; it need not be original or new—sometimes, indeed, it is some one else's thought which touches the train which seems so difficult to fire. But it must be sincere; one's very own; if one does not originate it one must, at least, give it the impress of one's own inmost mind.

Of course, even then the thing may not win acceptance; for a thought to appeal to others a certain sympathy must be abroad; there must be, to use a musical metaphor, a certain descant or accompaniment going on, into which one can drop one's music as an organist plays a solo, which gives voice and individuality to some quiet, gliding strain.

But the thing to remember is that the one condition of art is that the thought and the expression must be individual and absolutely sincere. To be accepted matters little, if only you have said what is in your heart.

Of course, many things must be combined as well—style, magic of word-painting, harmony, beauty. There are many people whose strong and sincere thoughts cannot be uttered, because they have no power of expression; but even these are all personality too.

There must be no deep and vital despondency in the artist's heart as to his right and power to speak. His duty is to gain flexibility by perseverance;

and, meanwhile, to analyse, to keep his mind large and sympathetic, to open all the windows of his heart to the day; not to be conventional, prejudiced, or wilful; to believe that any one who can see beauty or truth in a thing is nearer to its essence than one who can only criticise or despise.

This is roughly and awkwardly put; but I believe it to be true. Tell me what you feel about it; stay me with flagons, whatever that mysterious process may be....—Ever yours,

T. B.

OXFORD,
Dec. 23, 1904.

MY DEAR HERBERT,—I came down, as soon as the term was over, to Oxford, where I have come in the way of a good deal of talk. I find that I become somewhat of a connoisseur in the matter of conversation as I grow older; and I must also confess that such powers as I possess in that direction are of the tete-a-tete order. A candid friend of mine, a gracious lady, who wields some of the arts of a salon, lately took the wind out of my sails, on an occasion when I formed one of a large and rather tongue-tied party at her house. I had flung myself, rather strenuously, into the breach, and had talked with more valour than discretion. Later in the evening I had a little confabulation with herself, at the end of which she said to me, with a vaguely reminiscent air, "What a pity it is that you are only a tete-a-tete talker!"

To be a salon talker indeed requires a certain self-possession, a kind of grasp of the different individuals which surround you, which is of the nature of Napoleonic strategy.

At Oxford one does not find much general conversation. The party which meets night by night in Hall is too large for any diffused talk; and, moreover, the clink and clash of service, the merry chatter of the undergraduates fill the scene with a background of noise. There is a certain not unpleasant excitement, of the gambling type, as to who one's neighbours will be. Sometimes by a dexterous stroke one can secure one's chosen companion; but it also may happen that one may be at the end of the row of the first detachment which sits down to dinner (for the table slowly fills), and then it is like a game of dominoes; it is uncertain who may occupy one's nether flank. But the party is so large that there is a great variety. Of course we have our drawbacks—what society has not? There is the argumentative, hair-splitting Professor, who is never happy unless he is landing you in a false position and ruthlessly demolishing it. There is the crusted old Don, whose boots creak, whose clothes seem to be made of some hard, unyielding material, and whose stiff collars scrape his shaven cheeks with a rustling noise; he speaks rarely and gruffly; he opens his mouth to insert food, and closes it with a snap; but he is a humorous old fellow, with a twinkle in his eye; generous if whimsical; and more good-natured than he wishes you to believe. Some of my friends are silent and abrupt; there is the statuesque chaplain who, whatever you may talk of, appears to be preoccupied with something else; there are brisk, bird-like men, who pick up their food and interject disconnected remarks. But the majority are lively, sensible fellows, with abundance of interest in life and people, and a considerable sense of humour; and, after all, I think it matters very little what a man talks about as long as you feel that the talk is sincere and natural, and not a pose; the only kind of talker whom I find really discomposing is the shy man, who makes false starts, interrupts in order to show his sympathy, and then apologises for his misapprehension; but this is an unknown species in a College Hall. What one does weary of more and more every year is the sort of surface cackle that has to be indulged in in general society, simply to fill the time.

But of course, in conversation, much depends upon what may be called LUCK. You may invite three or four of the best conversationalists you know to a quiet dinner; and yet, though the same party may have on some previous occasion played the game with agility and zest, yet for some reason, on the present occasion, all may go heavily. You may light upon a tiresome subject; your most infectious humorist may be tired or out of temper, and the whole thing may languish and droop; people may misunderstand each other, perversely or unintentionally; the dredge may bring up nothing but mud; a contagion of yawning may set in, and you are lost. Again, some party which has been assembled from motives of duty, and from which no species of social pleasure was expected, may turn out brisk, lively, and entertaining.

A good party should contain, if possible, a humorist, a sentimentalist, and a good-tempered butt; the only kind of men who should be rigidly excluded are the busy mocker, the despiser, the superior person. It does not matter how much people disagree, if they will only admit in their minds that every one has a right to a point of view, and that their own does not necessarily rule out all others. I had two friends once, a husband and wife, who had strong political views; the wife believed it probable that all Radicals were either wicked or stupid, but it was possible to argue the point with her; whereas the husband KNEW that any person who, however slightly, entertained Liberal views was a fool or a knave, and thus argument was impossible.

Of course, there are a very few people who have a genius for conversation. Such persons are not as a rule great talkers themselves, though they every now and then emit a flash of soft brilliance; but they are rather the people who send every one else away contented; who see the possibilities in every remark; who want to know what other people think; and who can, by some deft sympathetic process which is to me very mysterious, expand a blunt expression of opinion into an interesting mental horizon, or fructify some faltering thought into a suggestive and affecting image. Such people are worth their weight in gold. Then there is a talker who is worth much silver, a man of irresistible geniality, who has a fund of pleasant banter for all present. This is a great art; banter, to be agreeable, must be of a complimentary kind; it must magnify the object it deals with—a perverse person may be bantered on his strength of character; a stingy person may be bantered on his prudence. There is, indeed, a kind of banter, not unknown in academical circles, which takes the heart out of every one by displaying them in a ludicrous and depreciating light; a professor of this art will make out a sensitive person to be a coward, and a poetical man to be a sentimental fool; and then the conversation, "like a fountain's sickening pulse, retires."

The talker who is worth much copper is the good, commonplace, courteous person who keeps up an end and has something to say; and these must be the basis of most parties—the lettuce, so to speak, of the salad.

The thing to beware of is to assemble a purely youthful party, unless you know your men well; a shy, awkward young man, or a noisy, complacent young man, are each in their way distressing. But a mixture of youth and age will produce the happiest results, if only your luck does not desert you.

After all, the essence of the thing is to have simple, unaffected people; the poseur is the ruin of genial intercourse, unless he is a good fellow whose pose is harmless. Some of the best talks I have ever had have been in the company of sensible and good-natured men, of no particular brilliance, but with a sense of justice in the matter of talk and no taste for anecdote; just as some of the best meals I have ever had have been of the plainest, when good digestion waited upon appetite. And, on the other hand, some of the very saddest entertainments I have ever taken a hand in have been those conducted by a host bubbling with geniality, and with a stock of reminiscences, who turned the hose in the face of guest after guest till they writhed with boredom.

Bless me, it is midnight! The hour is pealed from innumerable towers; then comes a holy silence, while I hear the drip of the fountain in the court. This incomparable Oxford! I wish that fate or Providence would turn my steps this way!—Ever yours,

T. B.

PELHAM HOUSE,
HAMMERSMITH,
Dec. 28, 1904.

DEAR HERBERT,—Since I left Oxford, I have been staying in town. I can't remember if you ever came across my old friend Hardy—Augustus Hardy, the art critic—at all events you will know whom I mean. I have been very much interested and a good deal distressed by my visit. Hardy is an elderly man now, nearly sixty. He went through Oxford with a good deal of distinction, and his sketches were much admired. It was supposed that he had only to present himself at the doors of the Academy, and that it would surrender at discretion. His family were rich, and Hardy went up to town to practise art. He was a friend of my father's, and he was very kind to me as a boy. He was well off, and lived in a pleasant house of his own in Half Moon Street. He was a great hero of mine in those days; he had given up all idea of doing anything great as a painter, but turned his attention to art-criticism. He wrote an easy, interesting style, and he used to contribute to magazines on all kinds of aesthetic subjects; he belonged to several clubs, dined out a great deal, and used to give elaborate little dinners himself. He was fond of lecturing and speechifying generally; and he liked the society of young people, young men of an intelligent and progressive type. He was very free with his money—I suppose he had nearly three thousand a year—and spent it in a princely kind of way; when he travelled he travelled like a great gentleman, generally took a young artist or two with him in whom he was interested, and whose expenses he paid.

He was in those days an admirable talker, quick, suggestive, amusing, and with an indefinable charm. He was then a tall, thin, active man, with flashing eyes, a sanguine complexion, and a mobile face; he wore his hair rather luxuriantly, and had a picturesque, pointed beard. I shall never forget the delight of occasional visits to his house; he was extraordinarily kind and really sympathetic, and he had with young people a kind of caressing deference in his manner that used to give one an agreeable sense of dignity. I remember that he had a very deft way of giving one's halting remarks a kind of twist which used to make it appear that one had said something profound and poetical.

Well, about twenty years ago, all this came to an end very suddenly. Hardy lost the greater part of his money at one swoop; he had inherited, I think, a certain share in his father's business; he had one brother, older than himself, who carried the business on. Hardy never looked into money matters, but simply spent whatever came in; the business came to grief, and Hardy found himself pretty considerably in debt, with a few hundreds a year of his own. He had, fortunately for himself, never married; his friends came to his assistance, and arranged matters as comfortably as possible. Hardy settled in an old house in Hammersmith, and has lived there ever since. He belonged to several clubs; but he resigned his membership of all but one, where he now practically spends his day, and having been always accustomed to have his own way, and dominate the societies in which he found himself, took it for granted that he would be the chief person there. He was always an egoist, but his position, his generosity, and his own charm had rather tended to conceal the fact.

Well, he has found every one against him in his adversity, and has suffered from all the petty intrigues of a small and rather narrow-minded society. His suggestions have been scouted, he has been pointedly excluded from all share in the management of the club, and treated with scanty civility. I don't suppose that all this has given him as much pain as one would imagine, because he has all the impenetrability and want of perception of the real egoist. I am told that he used to be treated at one time in the club with indifference, hostility, and even brutality. But he is not a man to be suppressed—he works hard, writes reviews, articles, and books, and pays elaborate civilities to all new members. I have only seen him at long intervals of late years; but he has stayed with me once or twice, and has often pressed me to go and see him in town. I had some business to attend there this Christmas, and I proposed myself. He wrote a letter of cordial welcome, and I have now been his guest for four days.

I can't express to you the poignant distress which my visit has caused me; not exactly a personal distress, for Hardy is not a man to be directly pitied; but the pathos of the whole thing is very great. His house has large and beautiful rooms, and I recognised many of the little treasures—portraits, engravings, statuettes, busts, and books—which used to adorn the house in Half Moon Street. But the man himself! He has altered very little in personal appearance. He still moves briskly, and, except that his hair is nearly white, I could imagine him to be the same hero that I used to worship. But his egoism has grown upon him to such an extent that his mind is hardly recognisable. He still talks brilliantly and suggestively at times; and I find myself every now and then amazed by some stroke of genius in his talk, some familiar thing shown in a new and interesting light, some ray of poetry or emotion thrown on to some dusty and well-known subject. But he has become a man of grievances; he still has, at the beginning of a talk, some of the fine charm of sympathy. He will begin by saying that he wants to know what one thinks of a point, and he will smile in the old affectionate kind of way, as one might smile at a favourite child; but he will then plunge into a fiery monologue about his ambitions and his work. He declaims away, with magnificent gestures. He still interlards his talk with personal appeals for approbation, for concurrence, for encouragement; but it is clear he does not expect an answer, and his demands for sympathy have little more personal value than the reiterated statement in the Litany that we are miserable sinners has in the mouth of many respectable church-goers.

The result is that I find myself greatly fatigued by my visit. I have spent several hours of every day in his society, and I do not suppose that I have uttered a dozen consecutive words; yet many of his statements would be well worth discussing, if he were capable of discussion.

The burden of his song is the lack of that due recognition which he ought to receive; and this, paradoxical as it may appear, is combined with an intense and childish complacency in his own greatness, his position, his influence, his literary and artistic achievements.

He seems to live a very lonely life, though a full one; every hour of his day is methodically mapped out. He has a large correspondence, he reads the papers diligently, he talks, he writes; but he seems to have no friends and no associates. His criticisms upon art, which are suggestive enough, are regarded with undisguised contempt by professional critics; and I find that they are held to be vitiated by a certain want of balance and proportion, and a whimsical eclecticism of taste.

But the pathos of the situation is not the opinion which is held of him, for he is wholly unconscious of it, and he makes up for any lack of expressed approbation by the earnest and admiring approval of all he does, which he himself liberally supplies. It is rather a gnawing hunger of the soul from which he seems to suffer; he has a simply boundless appetite for the poor thing which he calls recognition—I shudder to think how often I have heard the word on his lips—and his own self-approbation is like a drug which he administers to still some fretting pain.

He has been telling me to-night a long story of machinations against him in the club; the perspicacity with which he detected them, the odious repartees he made, the effective counter-checks he applied. "I was always a combatant," he says, with a leering gaiety. Then the next moment he is girding at the whole crew for their stupidity, their ingratitude, their malignity; and it never seems to cross his mind that he can be, or has been in the smallest degree, to blame. It distressed me profoundly, and my mind and heart seemed to weep silent tears.

If he had shown tact, prudence, diligence, if he could have held his tongue when he first took a different place, he would have had a circle of many friends by now. Instead of this, I find him barely tolerated. He talks—he has plenty of courage, and no idea of being put down—but he is listened to with ill-concealed weariness, and, at best, with polite indifference. Yet every now and then the old spell falls on me, and I realise what a noble mind is overthrown. He ought to be at this time the centre of a set of attached friends, a man spoken of with reverence, believed in, revisited by grateful admirers—a man whom it would be an honour and a delight to a young man to know; and the setting in which he lives is precisely adapted to this role. Instead of which it may safely be said that, if he were to announce his departure from town, it would be received with general and cordial satisfaction by his fellow-clubmen.

Even if he had not his circle, he might live a quiet, tranquil, and laborious life in surroundings which are simple and yet dignified.

But the poison is in his system, and it afflicts me to think in how many systems the same poison is at work nowadays. One sees the frankest form of it in the desire of third-rate people to amass letters after their names; but, putting aside all mere vulgar manifestations of it, how many of us are content to do good, solid, beautiful work unpraised, unsung, unheeded? I will take my own case, and frankly confess that what is called recognition is a pleasure to me. I like to have work, which I have done with energy, enjoyment, and diligence, praised—I hope because it confirms the verdict of my own mind that it has been faithfully done. But I can also sincerely say that, as far as literary work goes, the chief pleasure lies in the doing of it; and I could write with unabated zest even if there were no question of publication in view—at least, I think so, but one does not know oneself.

In any event, the contemplation of poor Hardy's case is a terrible lesson to one not to let the desire for praise get too strong a hold, or, at all events, to be deliberately on one's guard against it.

But the pathos and sadness, after all, remain. "Healing is well," says the poet, "but wherefore wounds to heal?" and I find myself lost in a miserable wonder under what law it is that the Creator can mould so fine a spirit, endow it with such splendid qualities, and then allow some creeping fault to obscure it gradually, as the shadow creeps over the moon, and to plunge it into disastrous and dishonourable eclipse.

But I grow tedious; I am inoculated by Hardy's fault. I hastily close this letter, with all friendly greetings. "Pray accept a blessing!" as little Miss Flite said. I am going down to my sister's to-morrow.—Ever yours,

T. B.

SIBTHORPE VICARAGE, WELLS,
Dec. 31, 1904 (and Jan. 1, 1905).

DEAR HERBERT,—It is nearly midnight, and I am sitting alone in my room, by the deathbed of the Old Year, expecting every moment to hear the bells break out proclaiming the birth of the New. It is a clear, still night, and I can see, beyond the lawn and over the shrubs of the Vicarage garden, by the light of a low moon, entangled in cloud, the high elms, the church tower, with a light in the belfry, like a solemn, cheerful eye, and the roofs of the little village, all in a patient, musing slumber. Everything is unutterably fresh, tranquil, and serene. By day it is a commonplace scene enough, with a sense of little work-a-day cares and businesses about it all; but now, at night, it is all dim and rich and romantic, full of a calm mystery, hushed and secret, dreaming contented dreams.

I have had an almost solitary day, except for meals. I like being here in a way; there is no strain about it. That is the best of blood-relationship; there is no need to entertain or to be entertained. My brother-in-law, Charles, is an excellent fellow, full to the brim of small plans and designs for his parish; my sister is a very simple and unworldly person, entirely devoted to her husband and children. My nephews and nieces, four in number, three girls and a boy, do not, I regret to say, interest me very deeply; they are amiable, healthy children, with a confined horizon, rather stolid; they never seem to quarrel or to have any particular preferences. The boy, who is the youngest, is to come to my house at Upton when he is old enough; but at present I am simply a good-natured uncle to the children, whose arrival and whose gifts make a pleasant little excitement. Our talk is purely local, and I make it my business to be interested. It is all certainly very restful. Sometimes—as a rule, in fact—when I stay in other people's houses, I have a sense of effort; I feel dimly that a certain brightness is expected of me; as I dress in the morning I wonder what we shall talk about, and what on earth I shall do between breakfast and lunch. But here I have a fire in my bedroom all day, and for the first time, I am permitted to smoke there. I read and write all the morning; I walk, generally alone, in the afternoon. I write before dinner. The result is that I am perfectly content. I sleep like a top; and I find myself full of ideas. The comfort of the whole thing is that no one is afraid that I am not amused, and I myself do not have the uneasy sense that I am bound, so to speak, to pay for my entertainment by being brisk, lively, or sympathetic. The immediate consequence is, that I get as near to all three qualities as I ever get. We simply live our own lives quietly, in company. My presence gives a little fillip to the proceedings; and I myself get all the benefit of change of scene, together with simple unexhausting companionship.

Hark! it is midnight! The soft murmur of bells rises on the clear air, toppling over in a sweet cascade of sound, bringing hope and peace to the heart. In the attic above I hear the children moving softly about, and catch the echo of young voices. They are supposed to be asleep, but I gather that they have been under a vow to keep awake in turn, the watcher to rouse the others just before midnight. The bells peal on, coming in faint gusts of sound, now loud, now low.

I suppose if I were more simple-minded I should have been thinking over my faults and failures, desiring to do better, making good resolutions. But I don't do that. I do desire, with all my heart, to do better. I know how faltering, how near the ground my flight is. But these formal, occasional repentances are useless things; resolutions do little but reveal one's weakness more patently. What I try to do is simply to uplift my heart with all its hopes and weaknesses to God, to try to put my hand in His, to pray that I may use the chances He gives me, and interpret the sorrows He may send me. He knows me utterly and entirely, my faults and my strength. I cannot fly from Him though I take the wings of the morning. I only pray that I may not harden my heart; that I may be sought and found; that I may have the courage I need. All that I have of good He has given me; and as for the evil, He knows best why I am tempted, why I fall, though I would not. There is no strength like the abasement of weakness; no power like a childlike confidence. One thing only I shall do before I sleep—give a thought to all I love and hold dear, my kin, my friends, and most of all, my boys: I shall remember each, and, while I commend them to the keeping of God, I shall pray that they may not suffer through any neglect or carelessness of my own. It is not, after all, a question of the quantity of what we do, but of the quality of it. God knows and I know of how poor a stuff our dreams and deeds are woven; but if it is the best we can give, if we desire with all our hearts what is noble and pure and beautiful and true—or even desire to desire it—He will accept the will and purify the deed. And in such a mood as this—and God forgive us for not more often dwelling in such thoughts—I can hope and feel that the most tragic failure, the darkest sorrow, the deepest shame are viewed by God, and will some day be viewed by ourselves, in a light which will make all things new; and that just as we look back on our childish griefs with a smiling wonder, so we shall some day look back on our mature and dreary sufferings with a tender and wistful air, marvelling that we could be so short-sighted, so faithless, so blind.

And yet the thought of what the new year may hold for us cannot be other than solemn. Like men on the eve of a great voyage, we know not what may be in store, what shifting of scene, what loss, what grief, what shadow of death. And then, again, the same grave peace flows in upon the mind, as the bells ring out their sweet refrain, "It is He that hath made us." Can we not rest in that?

What I hope more and more to do is to withdraw myself from material aims and desires; not to aim at success, or dignity of office, or parade of place. I wish to help, to serve, not to command or rule. I long to write a beautiful book, to put into words something of the sense of peace, of beauty and mystery, which visits me from time to time. Every one has, I think, something of the heavenly treasure in their hearts, something that makes them glad, that makes them smile when they are alone; I want to share that with others, not to keep it to myself. I drift, alas, upon an unknown sea; but sometimes I see, across the blue rollers, the cliffs and shores of an unknown land, perfectly and impossibly beautiful. Sometimes the current bears me away from it; sometimes it is veiled in cloud-drift and weeping rain. But there are days when the sun shines bright upon the leaping waves, and the wind fills the sail and bears me thither. It is of that beautiful land that I would speak, its pure outlines, its crag-hollows, its rolling downs. Tendimus ad Latium, we steer to the land of hope.

And meanwhile I desire but to work in a corner; to make the few lives that touch my own a little happier and braver; to give of my best, to withhold what is base and poor. There is abundance of evil, of weakness, of ugliness, of dreariness in my own heart; I only pray that I may keep it there, not let it escape, not let it flow into other lives.

The great danger of all natures like my own, which have a touch of what is, I suppose, the artistic temperament, is a certain hardness, a self-centred egotism, a want of lovingness and sympathy. One sees things so clearly, one hankers so after the power of translating and expressing emotion and beauty, that the danger is of losing proportion, of subordinating everything to the personal value of experience. From this danger, which is only too plain to me, I humbly desire to escape; it is all the more dangerous when one has the power, as I am aware I have, of entering swiftly and easily into intimate personal relations with people; one is so apt, in the pleasure of observing, of classifying, of scrutinising varieties of temperament, to use that power only to please and amuse oneself. What one ought to aim at is not the establishment of personal influence, not the perverted sense of power which the consciousness of a hold over other lives gives one, but to share such good things as one possesses, to assist rather than to sway.

Well, it is all in the hands of God; again and again one returns to that, as the bird after its flight in remote fields returns to the familiar tree, the branching fastness. One should learn, I am sure, to live for the day and in the day; not to lose oneself in anxieties and schemes and aims; not to be overshadowed by distant terrors and far-off hopes, but to say, "To-day is given me for my own; let me use it, let me live in it." One's immediate duty is happily, as a rule, clear enough. "Do the next thing," says the old shrewd motto.

The bells cease in the tower, leaving a satisfied stillness. The fire winks and rustles in the grate; a faint wind shivers and rustles down the garden paths, sighing for the dawn. I grow weary.

Herbert, I must say "Good-night." God keep and guard you, my old and true friend. I have rejoiced week by week to hear of your recovered health, your activity, your renewed zest in life. When shall I welcome you back? I feel somehow that in these months of separation we have grown much nearer and closer together. We have been able to speak in our letters in a way that we have seldom been able to speak eye to eye. There is a pure gain. My heart goes out to you and yours; and at this moment I feel as if the dividing seas are nothing, and that we are close together in the great and loving heart of God.—Your ever affectionate,

T. B.

SIBTHORPE VICARAGE, WELLS,
Jan. 7, 1905.

DEAR HERBERT,—Four nights ago I dreamed a strange dream. I was in a big, well-furnished, airy room, with people moving about in it; I knew none of them, but we were on friendly terms, and talked and laughed together. Quite suddenly I was struck somewhere in the chest by some rough, large missile, fired, I thought, from a gun, though I heard no explosion; it pierced my ribs, and buried itself, I felt, in some vital part. I stumbled to a couch and fell upon it; some one came to raise me, and I was aware that other persons ran hither and thither seeking, I thought, for medical aid and remedies. I knew within myself that my last hour had come; I was not in pain, but life and strength ebbed from me by swift degrees. I felt an intolerable sense of indignity in my helplessness, and an intense desire to be left alone that I might die in peace; death came fast upon me with clouded brain and fluttering breath....

SIBTHORPE VICARAGE, WELLS,
Jan. 7, 1905.

DEAR NELLIE,—I have just opened your letter, and you will know how my whole heart goes out to you. I cannot understand it, I cannot realise it; and I would give anything to be able to say a word that should bring you any comfort or help. God keep and sustain you, as I know He CAN sustain in these dark hours. I cannot write more to-day; but I send you the letter that I was writing, when your own letter came. It helps me even now to think that my dear Herbert told me himself—for that, I see, was the purpose of my dim dream—what was befalling him. And I am as sure as I can be of anything that he is with us, with you, still. Dear friend, if I could only be with you now; but you will know that my thoughts and prayers are with you every moment.—Ever your affectionate,

T. B.

[I add an extract from my Diary.—T. B.]

Diary, Jan. 15.—A week ago, while I was writing the above unfinished lines, I received a letter to say that my friend Herbert was dead—he to whom these letters have been written. It seems that he had been getting, to all appearances, better; that he had had no renewed threatenings of the complaint that had made him an exile. But, rising from his chair in the course of the evening, he had cried out faintly; put his hand to his breast; fallen back in his chair unconscious, and, in a few minutes, had ceased to breathe. They say it was a sudden heart-failure.

It is as though we had been watching by a burrow with all precaution that some little hunted creature should not escape, and that, while we watched and devised, it had slipped off by some other outlet the very existence of which we had not suspected.

Of course, as far as he himself is concerned, such a death is simply a piece of good fortune. If I could know that such would be the manner of my own death, a real weight would be lifted from my mind. To die quickly and suddenly, in all the activity of life, in comparative tranquillity, with none of the hideous apparatus of the sick-room about one, with no dreary waiting for death, that is a great joy. But for his wife and his poor girls! To have had no last word, no conscious look from one whose delicate consideration for others was so marked a part of his nature, this is a terrible and stupefying misery.

I cannot, of course, even dimly realise what has happened; the remoteness of it all, the knowledge that my own outer life is absolutely unchanged, that the days will flow on as usual, makes it trebly difficult to feel what has befallen me. I cannot think of him as dead and silent; yet even before I heard the news, he was buried. I cannot, of course, help feeling that the struggling spirit of my friend tried to fling me, as it were, some last message; or that I suffered with him, and shared his last conscious thought.

Perhaps I shall grow to think of Herbert as dead. But, meanwhile, I am preoccupied with one thought, that such an event ought not to come upon one as such a stunning and trembling shock as it does. It reveals to one the fact of how incomplete one's philosophy of life is. One ought, I feel, deliberately to reckon with death, and to discount it. It is, after all, the only certain future event in our lives.

And yet we struggle with it, put it away from us, live and plan as though it had no existence; or, if it insistently clouds our thoughts, as it does at intervals, we wait resignedly until the darkness lifts, and until we may resume our vivid interests again.

I do not, of course, mean that it should be a steady, melancholy preoccupation. If we have to die, we are also meant to live; but we ought to combine and co-ordinate the thought of it. It ought to take its place among the other great certainties of life, without weakening our hold upon the activity of existence. How is this possible? For the very terror of death lies not in the sad accidents of mortality, the stiffened and corrupting form, the dim eye, the dreadful pageantry—over that we can triumph; but it is the blank cessation of all that we know of life, the silence of the mind that loved us, the irreparable wound.

Some turn hungrily to Spiritualism to escape from this terrible mystery. But, so far as I have looked into Spiritualism, it seems to me only to have proved that, if any communication has ever been made from beyond the gate of death—and even such supposed phenomena are inextricably intertwined with quackeries and deceits—it is an abnormal and not a normal thing. The scientific evidence for the continuance of personal identity is nil; the only hope lies in the earnest desire of the hungering heart.

The spirit cries out that it dare not, it cannot cease to be. It cannot bear the thought of all the energy and activity of life proceeding in its accustomed course, deeds being done, words being uttered, the problems which the mind pondered being solved, the hopes which the heart cherished being realised—"and I not there." It is a ghastly obsession to think of all the things that one has loved best—quiet work, the sunset on familiar fields, well-known rooms, dear books, happy talk, fireside intercourse—and one's own place vacant, one's possessions dispersed among careless hands, eye and ear and voice sealed and dumb. And yet how strange it is that we should feel thus about the future, experience this dumb resentment at the thought that there should be a future in which one may bear no part, while we acquiesce so serenely in claiming no share in the great past of the world that enacted itself before we came into being. It never occurs to us to feel wronged because we had no conscious outlook upon the things that have been; why should we feel so unjustly used because our outlook may be closed upon the things that shall be hereafter? Why should we feel that the future somehow belongs to us, while we have no claim upon the past? It is a strange and bewildering mystery; but the fact that the whole of our nature cries out against extinction is the strongest argument that we shall yet be, for why put so intensely strong an instinct in the heart unless it is meant to be somehow satisfied?

Only one thought, and that a stern one, can help us—and that is the certainty that we are in stronger hands than our own. The sense of free-will, the consciousness of the possibility of effort, blinds us to this; we tend to mistake the ebullience of temperament for the deliberate choice of the will. Yet have we any choice at all? Science says no; while the mind, with no less instinctive certainty, cries out that we have a choice. Yet take some sharp crisis of life—say an overwhelming temptation. If we resist it, what is it but a resultant of many forces? Experience of past failures and past resolves combine with trivial and momentary motives to make us choose to resist. If we fail and yield, the motive is not strong enough. Yet we have the sense that we might have done differently: we blame ourselves, and not the past which made us ourselves.

But with death it is different. Here, if ever, falls the fiat of the Mind that bade us be. And thus the only way in which we can approach it is to put ourselves in dependence upon that Spirit. And the only course we can follow is this: not by endeavouring to anticipate in thought the moment of our end—that, perhaps, only adds to its terrors when it comes—but by resolutely and tenderly, day after day, learning to commend ourselves to the hand of God; to make what efforts we can; to do our best; to decide as simply and sincerely as possible what our path should be, and then to leave the issue humbly and quietly with God.

I do this, a little; it brings with it a wonderful tranquillity and peace. And the strange thing is that one does not do it oftener, when one has so often experienced its healing and strengthening power.

To live then thus; not to cherish far-off designs, or to plan life too eagerly; but to do what is given us to do as carefully as we can; to follow intuitions; to take gratefully the joys of life; to take its pains hopefully, always turning our hearts to the great and merciful Heart above us, which a thousand times over turns out to be more tender and pitiful than we had dared to hope. How far I am from this faith. And yet I see clearly that it is the only power that can sustain. For in such a moment of insight even the thought of the empty chair, the closed books, the disused pen, the sorrowing hearts, and the flower-strewn mound fail to blur the clear mirror of the mind.

For him there can be but two alternatives: either the spirit that we knew has lost the individuality that we knew and is merged again in the great vital force from which it was for a while separated; or else, under some conditions that we cannot dream of, the identity remains, free from the dreary material conditions, free to be what it desired to be; knowing perhaps the central peace which we know only by subtle emanations; seeing the region in which beauty, and truth, and purity, and justice, and high hopes, and virtue are at one; no longer baffled by delay, and drooping languor, and sad forebodings, but free and pure as viewless air.

THE END

Made in the USA
Monee, IL
23 June 2022

98497975R10092